WHY DID JESUS LIVE A PERFECT LIFE?

THE NECESSITY *of* CHRIST'S OBEDIENCE *for* OUR SALVATION

BRANDON D. CROWE

B
Baker Academic
a division of Baker Publishing Group
Grand Rapids, Michigan

© 2021 by Brandon D. Crowe

Published by Baker Academic
a division of Baker Publishing Group
PO Box 6287, Grand Rapids, MI 49516-6287
www.bakeracademic.com

Printed in the United States of America

Library of Congress Cataloging-in-Publication Data
Names: Crowe, Brandon D., author.
Title: Why did Jesus live a perfect life? : the necessity of Christ's obedience for our salvation / Brandon D. Crowe.
Description: Grand Rapids, Michigan : Baker Academic, a division of Baker Publishing Group, [2021] | Includes bibliographical references and index.
Identifiers: LCCN 2021023572 | ISBN 9781540962508 (paperback) | ISBN 9781540964526 (casebound) | ISBN 9781493432240 (ebook)
Subjects: LCSH: Obedience—Religious aspects—Christianity. | Salvation—Christianity.
Classification: LCC BV4647.O2 C76 2021 | DDC 248.4—dc23
LC record available at https://lccn.loc.gov/2021023572

Unless otherwise indicated, Scripture quotations are from The Holy Bible, English Standard Version® (ESV®), copyright © 2001 by Crossway, a publishing ministry of Good News Publishers. Used by permission. All rights reserved. ESV Text Edition: 2016

Baker Publishing Group publications use paper produced from sustainable forestry practices and post-consumer waste whenever possible.

21   22   23   24   25   26   27   7   6   5   4   3   2   1

For Mike and Lou

"Thy Works, Not Mine, O Christ"

Thy works, not mine, O Christ, speak gladness to
    this heart;
they tell me all is done; they bid my fear depart.
Thy pains, not mine, O Christ, upon the shameful
    tree,
have paid the law's full price and purchased peace
    for me.
Thy cross, not mine, O Christ, has borne the awful
    load
of sins that none in heav'n or earth could bear but
    God.
Thy righteousness, O Christ, alone can cover me:
no righteousness avails save that which is of thee.
To whom, save thee, who canst alone for sin atone,
Lord, shall I flee?

Horatius Bonar (1857)

CONTENTS

Contents

PREFACE

How does Jesus save his people from their sins? Following a long tradition, I argue that *perfect* obedience is necessary for salvation, and only Jesus meets this requirement. This does not belittle our own call to obedience, but our obedience is not the ground or basis of our acceptance before God.

This is not a new interpretation, but it has often been misunderstood and challenged. I hope to articulate this view clearly and to discuss some new angles as well. I have been addressing the topic of this book, in one way or another, for around fifteen years. It seemed fitting to bring much of the fruit of those labors together into a new, integrated, and sustained discussion for a wider audience. I am convinced that the obedience of Jesus is central to the theology of the New Testament and the Bible's teaching on redemption. I have done my best to limit the number of footnotes in this book in order to maximize readability and accessibility. Even so, I have included references (and sometimes quotations) where I follow an author in a particular way of framing a point or where an author has captured with particular clarity and precision the matters at hand. Sometimes we need to hear the older voices speaking for themselves.

Thanks to Bryan Dyer, Eric Salo, and the entire professional team at Baker Academic for supporting and shepherding another project through to completion. I express my gratitude to the trustees of Westminster Theological Seminary for granting a professional advancement leave in the first half of 2019, which allowed me to write the bulk of this manuscript. I am grateful for my colleagues at Westminster Seminary, who persistently encourage, teach, and challenge me with their wide-ranging expertises. I am also grateful for those who have served as conversation partners for this book and sharpened my own thinking. A special word of thanks goes to those who took the time to offer feedback on written portions of this manuscript, especially Todd Rester, Guy Waters, Dave Garner, Pip Mohr, and David Briones. Thanks also to Pip Mohr for compiling the indexes.

The love and support of my wife, Cheryl, are incalculably valuable. I also hope this book will be of interest to my children, though I trust I've covered the gist of the argument with them many times. I dedicate this book to my parents-in-law, Mike and Lou Webb, who have become like second parents. I am grateful for the godly legacy they have bequeathed to my wife and to our children. It is a great blessing to have loving, supportive parents; it is a double blessing to have loving, supporting in-laws as well. I have been doubly blessed.

ABBREVIATIONS

Greek and Latin Works

Apostolic Fathers

Diogn.   Epistle to Diognetus

Irenaeus of Lyons

Epid.   *Epideixis tou apostolikou kērygmatos (Demonstration of the Apostolic Preaching)*
Haer.   *Adversus haereses (Against Heresies)*

Justin Martyr

Dial.   *Dialogus cum Tryphone (Dialogue with Trypho)*

Francis Turretin

Inst.   *Institutes of Elenctic Theology.* Edited by James T. Dennison Jr. Translated by George Musgrave Giger. 3 vols. Phillipsburg, NJ: P&R, 1992–97

Modern Works

AB   Anchor Bible
AYB   Anchor Yale Bible
BBR   *Bulletin for Biblical Research*

Abbreviations

BDAG   Danker, Frederick W., Walter Bauer, William F. Arndt, and
        F. Wilbur Gingrich. *Greek-English Lexicon of the New
        Testament and Other Early Christian Literature.* 3rd ed.
        Chicago: University of Chicago Press, 2000
BECNT   Baker Exegetical Commentary on the New Testament
BZNW   Beihefte zur Zeitschrift für die neutestamentliche
        Wissenschaft
CCT   Contours of Christian Theology
COQG   Christian Origins and the Question of God
CTJ   *Calvin Theological Journal*
ESBT   Essential Studies in Biblical Theology
HC   Heidelberg Catechism, available at https://www.crcna.org
        /sites/default/files/Heidelberg%20Catechism_old.pdf
KJV   King James Version
LCC   Library of Christian Classics
LW   Luther, Martin. *Luther's Works.* Edited by Jaroslav
        Pelikan, Helmut T. Lehmann, and Christopher Brown.
        American ed. 82 vols. (projected). Philadelphia: Fortress;
        Saint Louis: Concordia, 1955–
NAC   New American Commentary
NICNT   New International Commentary on the New Testament
NIGTC   New International Greek Testament Commentary
NIV 1984 New International Version, 1984 version
NovTSup Supplements to Novum Testamentum
NTS   *New Testament Studies*
PPS   Popular Patristics Series
RD   Bavinck, Herman. *Reformed Dogmatics.* Edited by John
        Bolt. Translated by John Vriend. 4 vols. Grand Rapids:
        Baker Academic, 2003–8
SNTSMS Society for New Testament Studies Monograph Series
WBC   Word Biblical Commentary
WCF   Westminster Confession of Faith, in James T. Dennison
        Jr., ed., *Reformed Confessions of the Sixteenth and Seven-
        teenth Centuries in English Translation, 1523–1693*, 4 vols.
        (Grand Rapids: Reformation Heritage, 2008–14)
WLC   Westminster Larger Catechism, in James T. Dennison Jr.,
        ed., *Reformed Confessions of the Sixteenth and Seven-
        teenth Centuries in English Translation, 1523–1693*, 4 vols.
        (Grand Rapids: Reformation Heritage, 2008–14)
WSC   Westminster Shorter Catechism, in James T. Dennison Jr.,
        ed., *Reformed Confessions of the Sixteenth and Seven-
        teenth Centuries in English Translation, 1523–1693*, 4 vols.
        (Grand Rapids: Reformation Heritage, 2008–14)

WTJ	*Westminster Theological Journal*
WUNT	Wissenschaftliche Untersuchungen zum Neuen Testament
ZECNT	Zondervan Exegetical Commentary on the New Testament
ZNW	*Zeitschrift für die neutestamentliche Wissenschaft und die Kunde der älteren Kirche*

PART 1

DEFINITIONS

1

WHAT IS REQUIRED?

This is a book about Jesus and the salvation he has accomplished. But it's also a book about what is required of those who follow him as disciples. Surely these are two of the most important issues in life. Not surprisingly, these are questions on which there is much debate and disagreement. They are also complex questions that merit many volumes to address. Even so, there is a place for succinct and selective discussions of key issues, which is what I aim to do in this book.

The New Testament presents Jesus as the fully obedient Son of God. He is the perfect Savior who deals definitively with sin. On this, there is widespread agreement.

Yet the perfect obedience of Jesus receives less attention than one might expect in contemporary discussions of Jesus and salvation. When we turn to Scripture, the perfect obedience of Jesus is emphasized in the Gospels, Acts, Paul's Epistles, Hebrews, and elsewhere. The obedience of Jesus is also an emphasis of the early church, in writings that echo the New

Testament. If we want to understand the scriptural teaching on salvation, then the perfect obedience of Jesus is an important—if sometimes neglected—topic to consider.

In this book, my aim is to show anew some of the ways in which Jesus is a beautiful Savior and how we ought to live in response. I want to highlight ways in which his work is unique and how that informs what is required of his disciples.

Mounting Complexity

The issues covered in this book are complex. It's probably no surprise that debates on the doctrine of salvation are ongoing. To some, the questions have been settled hundreds of years ago. To others, we need a new Reformation in light of new insights from theology and biblical studies. This latter perspective is especially true for those following New Testament studies over the past forty years or so.

For example, for better or worse, one of the most disruptive developments in biblical studies pertaining to salvation in the past few decades is known as the New Perspective on Paul. Though this movement is diverse, in general it calls for a reassessment of Paul's theology, especially in light of a reassessment of ancient Jewish sources. This has been particularly pertinent for the doctrine of justification. Justification has been traditionally understood—in both Protestant and Roman Catholic circles—as the way a sinful person is made right before a holy God. According to some proponents of the New Perspective on Paul, however, justification has much less to do with "getting saved"—or with "getting in" to the covenant community. Instead, justification is about how people from very different backgrounds (i.e., Jew and gentile) dwell together as the people of God. In this sense, justification has more of a "horizontal" emphasis between people groups, rather than a "vertical" emphasis between individuals and God.

The New Perspective has sent shock waves across the landscape of biblical studies over the past few decades, and its tremors continue to be felt today. The dust of these debates has now settled quite a bit, but that doesn't mean that clarity abounds. Many are convinced by the newer proposals; many are not; and many are somewhere in between. The debates have also spilled over to other areas of New Testament interpretation. Despite a number of new insights into the apostle Paul that we've gained, I'm concerned that the New Perspective has led many not to greater clarity on the Bible's teaching of justification and the work of Christ, but to greater fogginess, waffling, and imprecision on matters that require precision and confidence.

The New Perspective is just one example. Another recent contribution argues that *faith* is best understood as *allegiance*, and thus we are saved by "allegiance alone."[1] Studies such as these require us to address some of the most pressing of all questions: How are sinners made right before a holy God? To what degree and in what way do our works play a role in salvation? Are we saved *entirely* on the basis of the work of another, or is it through some combination—however nuanced—of faith and our own works?

Intricate discussions on salvation and justification can quickly become complex, especially for those who encounter new arguments that challenge traditional views. (Sometimes you think you know something until you're asked to defend it.) This can lead to frustration and even a crisis of faith. What traditional points of understanding should stay? What should go? Is there a clear answer? Do the New Testament writers even agree on this question?

In the face of potential confusion about salvation, justification, and the work of Christ, I've found it helpful to focus on

---

1. Matthew W. Bates, *Salvation by Allegiance Alone: Rethinking Faith, Works, and the Gospel of Jesus the King* (Grand Rapids: Baker Academic, 2017).

one question—a question whose answer has far-reaching implications. It's a question that may seem obvious but is asked less often than you might think. One's answer to this question has a number of interrelated implications.

Piercing the Fog: One Key Question

The one key question that unlocks many of these debates, and one that helps explain the New Testament's emphasis on the obedience of Jesus Christ, is this: Is *perfect* obedience necessary for eternal life?

This question could be rephrased a number of ways: Is perfect obedience necessary for justification? Is perfect obedience necessary for salvation? Did Jesus *have* to be perfectly obedient in order to save us? And if so, why?

This is a simple question, but it's related to several other points, with which it forms an interconnected web. For example, one's answer to this question may determine the degree to which the New Perspective on Paul is compelling. If you believe that *perfect* obedience is necessary for salvation, then saying we are justified on the final day on the basis of our whole lives (as some New Perspective proponents argue) won't work.[2] If God requires perfect obedience, then even our best obedience is not adequate to meet the demands of God for eternal life.

Again, if you believe that *perfect* obedience is necessary for salvation, it will likely reveal what you believe about the biblical figure Adam. Was Adam required to be perfectly obedient? Was a covenant made with Adam? Even more fundamentally: Was Adam really the *first* person? Was Adam even a *real* person?

If you believe that *perfect* obedience is necessary for salvation, it will likewise reveal your approach to the Old Testament

---

2. See especially N. T. Wright, *Paul: In Fresh Perspective* (Minneapolis: Fortress, 2005), 121; for a more extended discussion and further nuance, see Wright, *Paul and the Faithfulness of God*, COQG 4 (Minneapolis: Fortress, 2013), 936–62.

law. How do the New Testament writers view the law? Are there layers of complexity in the use of the law in the New Testament? Is there room for understanding the law as God's gracious condescension to Israel *and* for viewing it as containing a principle requiring perfection for eternal life? Asking whether perfect obedience is necessary for salvation does not solve all debates, but it's an important compass to help keep our bearings in what can easily become a disorienting quagmire. This question also highlights a number of related issues that have to be addressed. For example, we cannot easily fudge on the question of the historical Adam, since, as I will show in following chapters, the need for perfect obedience has historically been traced back to the first man and what was required of him.

Answering the Question

To state the obvious, *asking* the question is not enough. We also need to investigate what answer the Bible gives to this question.

My answer to this key question is *yes*—the Bible does indeed teach that *perfect* obedience is necessary for salvation. If we miss this key point, we will have an impoverished understanding of what Christ does to save us. If we downplay or dispense with the idea that perfect obedience is necessary for salvation, we'll miss one of the key emphases of the New Testament, and thus the necessity and much of the beauty of Christ's work on our behalf. And if we miss this point, we will elevate our own works into an unworkable theological position.

In support of this claim, this book looks at select topics and texts from the New Testament with an eye to what is said about Jesus and the need for perfect obedience. I will discuss how and why Jesus is presented as the perfectly obedient Son of God and how we are to relate to him by faith. This is primarily a book about what Jesus has done, but it also touches on related areas such as faith, salvation, justification, and sanctification.

To be clear, this is not an exhaustive study of the work of Christ, Paul's theology, or justification. Far from it. This is a sketch in which I aim to provide a strategic set of windows that open up to some helpful vistas. These will draw our attention to some ways the New Testament highlights that the perfect obedience of Jesus is necessary for our salvation.

In this first part of the book, I clear the land by providing orienting discussions. In chapter 2 I clarify commonly used terminology related to the obedience of Jesus. Many people speak about the active and passive obedience of Jesus, but these terms are not widely understood. Even if one were to disagree with or quibble with this or that aspect of these traditional categories, we need to be clear on what we're talking about. Chapter 2 will thus bring much-needed clarity to the conversation. I argue that active and passive obedience are not two *stages* of Jesus's obedience, but two ways of describing his *unified* obedience, and both aspects are necessary for salvation. I also discuss the various benefits of justification, which correlate to the entire obedience of Jesus, and how justification relates to salvation.

Part 2 focuses on biblical texts. In chapter 3 I address one of the most consequential and debated aspects of the obedience of Jesus—the relationship of Jesus to Adam. In this chapter I give extended attention to Romans 5:12–21. Here it's clear that Paul understood Adam to be a real person. If we miss this relationship, or if we downplay the reality of Adam as the head of the human race, then much of the New Testament's portrait of Jesus and his work will crumble. I will also seek to show that the obedience required of Adam was comprehensive, and not limited to one command.

Chapter 4 considers what the New Testament says about the law of Moses, asking, specifically: Did the Mosaic law require perfect obedience? Wasn't it given to a redeemed people? Didn't it provide ways to atone for sin? I will argue that a full answer to this question must relate the law of Moses to Adam. The Mosaic law was indeed given to a redeemed people, yet it still echoes the need for perfect obedience if one were to seek life by means of works. Here I will address the complicated use of Leviticus 18:5 in the New Testament, including in Luke 10, Romans 10, and Galatians 3.

Chapter 5 looks to the Gospels, where the perfect life of Jesus is narrated. In the Gospels Jesus is consistently presented as the fully obedient, representative Son of God, who, by his obedience, accomplishes salvation. His people therefore should trust in him, that they may have life. In other words—in the Gospels, the obedience of Jesus benefits his people. Key texts include Jesus's baptism, temptation, the Lord's Prayer, the binding of the strong man, and union with Christ in the Gospel of John.

Chapter 6 turns to Hebrews and considers the sacrifice of Jesus as high priest. Focusing particularly on the incarnation and the use of Psalm 40 in Hebrews 10, I will show that Jesus could only serve as an effective and final high priest by doing all that God commands, and thus overcoming the dichotomy between sacrifice and obedience that was so often a problem for God's covenant people.

Chapter 7 considers the implications of Jesus's resurrection for his obedience. Looking at the Gospels, Acts, and Paul's Letters, I will show that the logic of the resurrection requires and assumes Jesus's perfect obedience. The resurrection proves that Jesus never sinned and that he entirely, always, fully did the will of God. Since the resurrection is necessary for salvation, this means that Jesus's perfect obedience is necessary for salvation.

Part 3 turns to practical application. In chapters 8–9 I relate these issues to justification and Christian discipleship. What is required of followers of Jesus? If Jesus is the perfectly obedient Savior, and if his perfect obedience is necessary for salvation, then what is the role of our imperfect works? Is our obedience optional? Should we say our obedience is *necessary*? If so, does this undermine the role of Jesus's perfect obedience? These are important questions. Thankfully, they're also questions that have been dealt with at length, and I think decisively, in the history of Christian exegesis. More importantly, these are issues that are addressed sufficiently in the New Testament itself. I conclude briefly in chapter 10 with some final observations.

Finding the Right Recipe: Biblical, Historical, and Systematic Theology

Keeping the "Biblical" in Biblical Theology

One of the reasons I think that this question—Is perfect obedience necessary?—has become so murky in recent years is an overemphasis on a limited subset of New Testament writings. For example, instead of asking, "What does the New Testament teach?," a great many studies focus on what Matthew, Mark, or Luke says. This is often what is in mind when someone thinks of "biblical theology."

On the one hand, focusing on the contributions of specific biblical authors is legitimate and is an approach that I have often used myself. On the other hand, this approach has significant limitations, especially if it is the staple of our diet of biblical interpretation. A biblical theology consisting of one text (or one author) is not sufficient; such an approach doesn't deal with all the riches of revelation we have on a given topic. We therefore need to be circumspect about this corpus-by-corpus or author-by-author approach. This approach tends to separate biblical writings from one another rather than synthesizing them. For those who hold to the sufficiency of Scripture, it is important to recognize the need for *all* the Scriptures in order to have a sufficient picture of any theological issue.

To be sure, this is not the *only* way to do things. A corpus-by-corpus approach may be used for a variety of reasons. Some use this approach because they find in the New Testament irreconcilable diversity among its writings, leading to the need to prioritize certain writings over others. Some even find irreconcilable diversity among the thirteen letters of the Pauline corpus. Indeed, it is standard in many circles of New Testament scholarship today to deal mainly with a subset of the traditional thirteen Pauline Letters—normally around seven of them—due to the theory that Paul did not really write all of them. Despite the popularity of this method in recent years, it's a relatively novel approach that deviates in significant ways from the early witness of the church. It also assumes much of what it seeks to prove—not least by viewing diversity in the New Testament as *irreconcilable* diversity.

Others study discrete units of the New Testament for better reasons, such as the need to hear each author on his own terms, the need to deal with a more limited corpus because of how complex the issues are, the desire to study one book of the Bible as deeply as possible, and so forth. As I've said, this is a legitimate approach. Yet if this is the staple of our diet—if this is all we ever do—it can be unhealthy. We also need studies that synthesize the biblical texts and assume fundamental unity across the biblical writers' perspectives. We need studies that look at all thirteen of Paul's Letters alongside all four Gospels. We need studies that look at both James and Galatians. We need studies that don't bifurcate between the writings of Paul and Peter.

In this book, I will therefore look across the landscape of the New Testament. I assume a fundamental unity of the New Testament (and Old Testament) and believe it is not only legitimate but necessary to bring the New Testament voices together in a coherent way. Not every study has to take this approach, but it's important that some do. We also need the Old Testament. The New Testament grows organically out of the Old Testament, and the Old Testament witness is assumed and integral to the witness of the New Testament. To discuss the perfect work of Christ, therefore, requires us to consider the Old Testament as well.

Systematic and Historical Theology

In terms of historical and systematic theology, I am convinced that exegesis has often been done well in the history of the church, and we have much to learn from our exegetical predecessors. We need to engage the biblical texts anew today, but we should do so in light of what has been said in prior generations. Rarely are we the first to ask important and difficult questions of the biblical texts. It is wise to consider insights from previous generations.

I have often found it to be true that interpretive positions from the past, if they are indeed accurate interpretations, stand the test of time. We have certainly learned more about a whole host of things in recent decades, and sometimes older interpretations need to be modified. But surprisingly often, the best interpretation is already there somewhere in the history of interpretation, even if it could be nuanced further. As one New Testament scholar lamented, "Many of the best arguments in the history of interpretation have never been refuted, just forgotten or ignored."[3] I therefore interact liberally with systematic and historical theology wherever possible. I also do this to bring as much clarity as possible to terms that are often too nebulously understood today.

Combing and Combining Biblical, Historical, and Systematic Theology

I also believe that tradition is not the last word and that we need always to be looking to Scripture for new insights. This

3. Andreas J. Köstenberger, translator's preface to *The History of the Christ: The Foundation for New Testament Theology*, by Adolf Schlatter, trans. Andreas J. Köstenberger (Grand Rapids: Baker, 1997), 14.

is not, then, a book merely about what others have said. I also engage constructively in the task of exegesis to demonstrate in some fresh ways how the work of Christ is multifaceted—like a diamond. My primary focus is thus on biblical theology. Yet I believe that biblical theology is best done by ignoring artificial distinctions between historical, systematic, and biblical theology.

Many important questions have been raised in recent years, and it's not my aim either to minimize their difficulty or to provide a thorough discussion of—for example—the doctrine of justification. My concern is to highlight and appreciate the uniqueness of Christ's work. Though I often agree with the emphasis on Christian discipleship in some recent reassessments of the Bible's teaching on salvation, I fear that the baby has too often been thrown out with the bathwater. Traditional readings of Paul, for example, are not as exegetically thin as they have sometimes been made out to be. Though the "traditional" is not unassailable, typically the burden of proof should be on the newer insights to wrestle deeply with exegetical tradition. Whatever one's final conclusion on the matters covered here, I hope to bring clarity to the terms of the debate so that some strong voices in the exegetical tradition can be part of the discussion today. My method will therefore comb and combine biblical, historical, and systematic theology (with an emphasis on the *biblical*).

At the same time, this is not a book that is burdened with a large number of technical discussions. Many of the topics I address in this book I have written on in a more technical way in other venues. The footnotes that I include in what follows typically reflect particularly pertinent or important sources, or new sources I have not cited in earlier works.

Conclusion

Whether you've encountered recent debates or not, whether you're just now considering these issues or have considered them for many years, whether recent reformulations leave you convinced, resistant, or uncertain, in what follows I hope to advance the conversation and provide some new ways of thinking through the issues.

In short, my goal is to defend the position that Jesus's *perfect* obedience is necessary for eternal life, which is to say it is necessary for our salvation. This is not a matter of a few isolated prooftexts but is woven into the warp and woof of the New Testament in various ways, as we will see in what follows.

2

THE BASIS OF JUSTIFICATION

We were speaking the same language, but not talking about the same thing.

"You gave me *too many* burgers."

"Yes, I gave you *two mini* burgers."

I remember this frustrating encounter vividly. I was ordering dinner in the United Kingdom at a restaurant that was running a special on miniature cheeseburgers. These burgers came in sets of two. I ordered *one* set of two burgers, but received *two* sets of two burgers. I tried to communicate this to the cashier, but our conversation went nowhere fast. Adding to the confusion was my American Southern accent, which encountered his Eastern European accent in Scotland—a country with its own brand of English. In this case, I never succeeded in communicating what I meant.

How often do we talk past one another because we envision different things? Before diving more deeply into the interpretation of Scripture, it will be important at the outset to be clear about some important definitions. In this chapter I want to show a few things. First, I discuss justification, along with its basis or foundation. Second, I discuss the two aspects of Jesus's obedience: active and passive. These are crucial distinctions that must be understood with nuance. Third, I discuss how these two aspects of Jesus's obedience relate to the two benefits of justification.

In this chapter I lay the groundwork; in the chapters that follow I will defend my discussions and definitions more fully.

The Obedience of Jesus and Justification

Salvation and Justification

Salvation is a richly multifaceted term and difficult to summarize. One brief definition is deliverance from sin unto everlasting life in fellowship with the triune God. In this chapter and throughout much of this book, I will focus in large measure on a particular aspect of salvation—justification. Though salvation is broader than justification, justification is crucially important to salvation. This means that in order to understand salvation we must understand the doctrine of justification. Further, to understand justification rightly, we must appreciate how it relates to the obedience of Jesus himself.

Defining Justification

Historically, justification has often been closely tethered to the perfect obedience of Christ. But what is justification? To propose a definition is to invite disagreement. But in my view, the answer of the Westminster Shorter Catechism captures it extremely well. Though we have learned much in biblical studies since the seventeenth century, this remains one of the best definitions of *justification*. It is biblical, concise, and lucid. Though I do not aim here to provide a full defense of this definition, a few aspects of it merit brief explanation.

What Is Justification?

Q. What is justification?

A. Justification is an act of God's free grace wherein he pardons all our sins and accepts us as righteous in his sight, only for the righteousness of Christ imputed to us and received by faith alone.

—WSC (1647), question and answer 33
(slightly edited for modernization)

First, justification is an *act* of God's free grace: this means there is nothing a sinner can contribute to justification; God alone must act to justify a sinner. This focus on the divine act in justification can be compared to the definition of *sanctification* in the Westminster Shorter Catechism 35. Whereas justification is an *act* of God's free grace, sanctification is a *work* of God's free grace, which highlights the believer's responsibility to grow in grace (more on this in chapters 8–9). Put simply, justification is solely an act of God, whereas sanctification involves our works as well. The Shorter Catechism's question and answer on justification further highlights that justification is by faith *alone*, which means there are no works we can do to earn or to contribute to justification. Faith thus construed is not a *work*, but an *instrument*. I will also say more about this in future chapters.

Second, there are two aspects to justification: God (1) pardons all our sins and (2) accepts us as righteous in his sight. These two benefits are important for understanding the obedience of Jesus.

Third, the foundation or ground of our justification is the righteousness of Christ, which is used here as another way of speaking about the obedience of Christ. This means we are justified *on the basis of* Christ's perfect obedience, or his perfect *righteousness*. The obedience of Christ is broader than only his death on the cross; it includes all he did to realize God's righteous requirements for humanity. This is the ground, foundation, or basis of justification.

Fourth, the righteousness of Christ is *imputed* to believers by faith alone. The technical theological term *impute* is particularly significant for justification, as it guards the uniqueness of Christ's obedience. I will say more about the concept of imputation below.

In sum, justification refers to something God does for us apart from any work of our own, and it rests entirely on the perfect obedience of Jesus.

The Broad Scope of Jesus's Obedience

If the basis of justification is the perfect obedience of Jesus, this must be pursued further. How do we define and/or delimit the obedience of Christ? When we think of the obedience of Jesus, our thoughts may be directed first of all to the obedience of Jesus on the cross. This is indeed a biblical way to emphasize the obedience of Jesus. Jesus's death on the cross is often correlated to justification. In Romans 5:9, Paul states: "Since, therefore, we have now been *justified by [Jesus's] blood*, much more shall we be saved by him from the wrath of God." It is therefore not surprising that many have argued we are saved by the death (and resurrection) of Christ. This fits well with the New Testament emphasis on the centrality of the cross in relation to salvation (e.g., 1 Cor. 1:18; 2:2; Gal. 2:20; 6:14; Eph. 2:16; Phil. 2:8). Paul, in particular, clearly sees the cross of Christ to be central to salvation. In Romans 5:18, Paul even seems to say that we are saved by one act of righteousness: "Therefore, as one trespass led to condemnation for all men, so one act of righteousness leads to justification and life for all men." If one act of obedience leads to justification and life, then the most obvious, singular act of obedience is Jesus's faithfulness to death on the cross.

However, the matter is not quite so simple, for surely the obedience of Jesus extends beyond the cross as well. Jesus was obedient throughout his ministry, from his temptations in the wilderness to his testimony before the high priest on the final day of his life. Jesus even said that he always does what pleases his Father (John 8:29). Beyond this, as a child Jesus was obedient to his heavenly Father (Luke 2:49) and to his earthly parents (2:51). Historically many have recognized this widespread obedience of Jesus, inclusive of his whole life—not just his obedience on the cross—to be necessary for justification.

The terminology often used to describe the obedience of Jesus in this regard is the *active obedience* of Christ and the *passive obedience* of Christ. These terms must be understood properly. Some have argued that the passive obedience of Christ refers to Jesus's death, whereas active obedience refers to his life. Further, it is common to suggest that the passive obedience is necessary for justification, whereas the active obedience is more foreign to the New Testament.

However, we must be careful here. To *divide* the obedience of Jesus in any way is insufficient theologically and exegetically. It would not be correct to understand the passive obedience to refer to Jesus's death *only*, whereas his active obedience refers *only* to the obedience of his life. In fact, I believe that misunderstanding these terms has led to undue confusion not only about the obedience of Christ but also about justification and what is necessary for eternal life. We therefore need clear definitions of these terms that describe the *entire* obedience of Jesus, and we need to understand why the *entire* obedience of Jesus is necessary for justification.

The Active and Passive Obedience of Christ

We turn now to a fuller definition of the active obedience and passive obedience of Jesus Christ. Though few would quibble with the point that the New Testament presents Jesus as the perfectly obedient Savior, parsing this out in detail proves more

> ## Comparing and Contrasting Active Obedience and Passive Obedience
>
> | Active Obedience | Passive Obedience |
> | --- | --- |
> | Includes Jesus's entire life | Includes Jesus's entire life |
> | Includes Jesus's death | Includes Jesus's death |
> | Cannot be separated from passive obedience | Cannot be separated from active obedience |
> | Positive obedience to the law of God | Suffering the penal consequences of sin |
> | Correlates to the right to eternal life | Correlates to the forgiveness of sins |

complicated. Thankfully, we find a great deal of help in the history of exegesis in thinking through the issues related to Jesus's obedience and how this relates to justification. It is quite helpful to think of the obedience of Jesus having two aspects: active and passive. Simply put, active and passive obedience refer not to two different *stages* of obedience, but to two interrelated *aspects* of Jesus's unified obedience to the law of God as Mediator.

We begin with passive obedience, which often meets with less resistance. At the same time, in my experience this term is widely misunderstood. The passive obedience of Jesus refers to the suffering of Jesus—his bearing the penal effects of sin *throughout his incarnate life* as Mediator. The term can be misleading in English, since *passive* typically means that someone is receptive and inactive. However, though *passive obedience* has sometimes been taken to indicate Christ's passive acceptance of his death,[1] it is better to understand "pas-

1. See, e.g., Richard A. Muller, *Dictionary of Latin and Greek Theological Terms: Drawn Principally from Protestant Scholastic Theology*, 2nd ed. (Grand Rapids: Baker Academic, 2017), 237.

sive" to mean "to suffer" from the Latin *patior* (Greek: *paschein*). This correlates with a more extensive understanding of Christ's passive obedience that includes his entire life. To put the matter differently: Jesus's passive obedience was voluntary—it was *active* suffering. Jesus persevered in faithful obedience even when it was difficult—even to the point of death.

It's also crucial to note that the passive obedience was not limited to one climactic act or even one phase of Jesus's life. Passive obedience refers not only to the cross (though it does indeed climax on the cross) but also to the suffering Jesus endured throughout his *entire life* under the law of God. This period of life lived under the law—subject to sin, suffering, and death—is what theologians often call Jesus's estate of humiliation.

Active obedience likewise refers to Jesus's entire life—his perfect, positive accomplishment of all that God's law requires of humanity. This requires a bit more comment, since the term *law* can be used in so many different ways in Scripture. To be most precise, though Jesus came under the Mosaic administration of the law (Gal. 4:4), he ultimately had to do all that was required of Adam in the beginning—which was perfect obedience. Put simply, Jesus had to love and obey God fully.

It is also crucial to understand that while it would be easy to equate the passive obedience of Jesus with his suffering on the cross, and the active obedience of Jesus with his life before the cross, this does not do justice to the biblical teaching. These are not *temporal* distinctions. That is, *active* and *passive* obedience do not refer to two different phases of Jesus's life. To say so would be to divide the obedience of Christ in a way that Scripture does not. Instead, the active obedience and passive obedience are *logical* distinctions that describe two *aspects* of the unified obedience of Jesus. These two aspects always coincide in the lifelong, integrated, vicarious obedience of Jesus. Even so, it is important to make a logical distinction between the two. They are distinct but inseparable.

Let's tease this out a bit more. If the passive obedience of Christ is about the entire life of Jesus, this means the active obedience of Christ is also about Jesus's entire life—including his obedience in death. It would be a mistake to think of the death of Jesus as somehow *not* constituting his active obedience. For indeed, it is in the death of Christ that we see the obedience of Christ most dramatically. Additionally, Jesus's role as the Lamb of God who takes away the sin of the world (John 1:29; 1 Cor. 5:7) necessitates his entire sinlessness. For Jesus to be a spotless sacrifice he was required to do (positively) *all* that God requires. The law of God does not simply prohibit certain actions but also requires certain actions.

What is more, in the New Testament we find that the moral aspects of the law of God are much more demanding than many in Jesus's day seem to have thought (see Matt. 5:17–20; 7:12). Even the prohibitions of the law contain within them the requirement positively to act righteously. The law requires that we positively love God and neighbor (Matt. 22:37–40 and parallels; see also Lev. 19:18; Deut. 6:5). Or, as Matthew states twice in his Gospel, the Lord requires both mercy and sacrifice (Matt. 9:13; 12:7; see also Hosea 6:6). But we can take it a step further. For the law not only commands *external* actions but even demands *internal* obedience.[2] Who is sufficient for these things?

Jesus not only taught us these things; he lived them. Simply put, were Jesus to have failed to complete all of what God requires—by way of shorthand, fully loving God and neighbor—then he would not have been sinless, and therefore would not

---

2. Amandus Polanus von Polansdorf, *Syntagma Theologiae Christianae* (Hanover: Wechel, 1615), §6.10 (p. 350), §6.14 (p. 366).

have been qualified to serve as a perfect sacrifice. Justification rests on our Savior's entire, perfect obedience.

Though there has never been uniformity in the history of interpretation on the nature of Jesus's obedience, there is a long tradition that has carefully, systematically, and exegetically considered the matter, especially as it relates to justification. We cannot divide the obedience of Jesus.

This recognition of what the law of God requires and the indivisibility of Jesus's obedience relate directly to justification. For since the Bible teaches the possibility of justification, there must be a basis on which we can be justified before a holy God. That basis must be either the work of Christ alone or our works or some admixture of Christ's work and our works. The best answer is the work of Christ alone. Justification rests on the entire righteousness—or, perhaps better, the entire *obedience*—of Jesus Christ, active and passive.

This means we are not justified only on the basis of the death of Christ. Nor are we justified only on the basis of the passive obedience of Christ (which is not simply identified with his death). Certainly, the cross is central. However, we must take care to guard the unity of and appreciate the totality of Christ's obedience for justification. The entire, unified obedience of Jesus provides the ground of justification.

To be justified before God requires the active and passive obedience of Jesus. Jesus's entire obedience meets God's requirements. To risk oversimplification, we have two big problems: we are disqualified from eternal life because of sin, and we have not met the requirements positively for eternal life. Jesus's obedience addresses both these issues.

Two Benefits of Justification

This brings us to the two benefits of justification. Some may think of justification as the forgiveness of sins. But justification

23

Two Benefits of Justification

1. Right to eternal life: correlates to Jesus's *active obedience*
2. Forgiveness of sins: correlates to Jesus's *passive obedience*

is about more than only this. Justification is about both the forgiveness of sins and the right to eternal life. These two benefits of justification correspond to the two aspects of Jesus's obedience.[3]

First to consider is the forgiveness of sins. The law requires punishment for sin. Sin cannot simply be swept aside and forgotten without recompense. Sin brings a penalty, leading to death, for every person born naturally since Adam. That penalty must be paid.

This aspect of Jesus's obedience is not as controversial for those who recognize the need for forgiveness of sins through the death of Christ. However, a right understanding of passive obedience also tells us that Jesus bore the wrath of God throughout the whole course of his lifelong obedience. Jesus's passive obedience speaks to the penalty he paid throughout his life, which corresponds to the forgiveness of our sins in justification.

Second, to be justified we must also meet the positive requirements for eternal life. Justification consists of more than the forgiveness of sins. For if we are "only" forgiven for our disobedience, we still have not realized the positive requirements for eternal life. Attaining eternal life requires *perfect* obedience.

3. Adoption is also closely associated with the benefits of justification. See WCF 12.1; also 11.5.

Here we must consider Adam, who was promised eternal life on condition of his perfect obedience. Adam failed. However, we should not think that with Adam's failure the requirement of perfect obedience for eternal life is somehow swept away, as if with a wave of the hand. Instead, perfect obedience continued to be the requirement for the inheritance of eternal life. To be clear, this obedience must be perfect obedience, and not the obedience of believers in sanctification. As theologian Herman Bavinck persuasively argues:

> The works accomplished after justification by faith cannot be considered for justification, because then the order of redemption would be reversed and justification would be made dependent on sanctification, and also because those good works are still always imperfect and polluted by sin, and not in keeping with the full requirement of the divine law (Matt. 22:37; Gal. 3:10; James 2:10). God, being faithful and true, cannot view as perfect that which is not perfect. As the righteous and holy One, God cannot give up the demands of the law nor content

Heidelberg Catechism, Question and Answer 37: On Jesus's Lifelong Suffering

Q. What do you understand by the word "suffered"?
A. That during his whole life on earth, but especially at the end, Christ sustained in body and soul the anger of God against the sin of the whole human race. This he did in order that, by his suffering as the only atoning sacrifice, he might set us free, body and soul, from eternal condemnation, and gain for us God's grace, righteousness, and eternal life.

himself with a semirighteousness, which is basically no righteousness at all.[4]

For Bavinck, whose discussions draw widely from a variety of theological predecessors, eternal life requires perfect obedience to God's law. As I will argue in later chapters, appreciating the perfection of obedience required for eternal life is foundational for understanding the nature of justification in the New Testament and makes sense of why Jesus is so often portrayed as fully obedient in the New Testament.

It is also crucial to appreciate the historical reality of Adam and his uniqueness in world history. For in the Old Testament it is only with Adam in his sinless, created state that the possibility of eternal life upon the condition of perfect obedience, according to the covenant, is possible.[5] Once sin enters the world, it affects all those born naturally after Adam. Paul's argument in Romans 5 makes clear that Adam is a covenant head of humanity. As the first man, and a man with whom God entered into a special relationship, Adam's sinful actions affect those who come after him (Rom. 5:12). Although the Mosaic law later comes to Israel in the Old Testament, the Mosaic law is not given to a sinless people for whom perfect obedience is a possibility. The Israelites were never in a position to gain eternal life, strictly speaking, by their law keeping. God's grace preceded the giving of the Mosaic law; the Mosaic law was never intended as the means to secure eternal life. Only *perfect* obedience can meet the demands of eternal life; imperfect obedience simply will not suffice.

This is why we must start with Adam if we want to understand justification. Following the precedent of Paul, we must

---

4. Bavinck, *RD*, 4:209; see also Turretin, *Inst.*, 16.3.3 (2:647).
5. I discuss a possible covenant with Adam in ch. 3. I am not able to defend it at length here, but I believe the concept is present in Gen. 2–3 and is alluded to in Hosea 6:7. I provide further defense in *The Path of Faith: A Biblical Theology of Covenant and Law*, ESBT (Downers Grove, IL: IVP Academic, 2021), 11–17.

start at the beginning. To construe Paul's references to Adam in texts like Romans 5 and 1 Corinthians 15 as nonhistorical illustrations echoes not the apostle's thought, but the drumbeats of modernism. We are unlikely to understand justification biblically if we deny or downplay Adam. We must understand the problems confronting humanity in the beginning if we are to understand justification and the obedience of Jesus in the New Testament.

To summarize, Jesus's obedience can be understood to have active and passive dimensions, which correspond to the two benefits of justification. Forgiveness of sins corresponds to Christ's passive obedience, and the securing of eternal life corresponds to Christ's active obedience. Just as we must not artificially divide the passive and active obedience of Christ, neither must we divide the benefits of Christ's unified obedience, as if one could possess one without the other. Justification includes both forgiveness of sins and the right to eternal life. Likewise, it is not just "this" or "that" part of Jesus's obedience that provides the ground for justification; it is the *entire* obedience of Jesus that saves. As John Calvin memorably and succinctly stated: "How has Christ abolished sin, banished the separation between us and God, and acquired righteousness to render God favorable and kindly toward us? . . . He has achieved this by the whole course of his obedience."[6]

Justification and Imputation

Defining Imputation

When we ask how the obedience of Christ can be reckoned to us, the best answer is by means of *imputation*. This

---

6. John Calvin, *Institutes of the Christian Religion*, ed. John T. McNeill, trans. Ford Lewis Battles, 2 vols., LCC 20–21 (Philadelphia: Westminster, 1960), 2.16.5 (1:507); see also 3.11.2 (1:726–27).

is a technical and widely debated term, but it is an important term that reflects the teaching of Scripture (see Rom. 4:5) and accurately describes how Jesus's obedience benefits his people. In brief, imputation means that in justification the obedience of Christ—including both active and passive dimensions—is forensically (that is, legally) credited to believers by faith alone.

Imputation recognizes that the righteousness credited to believers in justification is entirely the righteousness of another. Since everyone born naturally after Adam is a sinner, no one can meet the requirements of eternal life; justification requires perfect obedience. Given Adam's role as the first, representative man, his sin has been imputed to all humanity born "in him." However, as the last Adam, born of a virgin, Jesus similarly stands at the head of a new humanity, and he is not affected by the guilt and corruption of Adam's sin. The remedy to the imputed sin of Adam comes by the last Adam, Jesus Christ, whose obedience is imputed to all who believe in him. It is important to understand that Adam was not bound simply to one command, but was called to be fully righteous and love God wholly. Therefore, the work of Jesus as the last Adam involves not only forgiving sins but also realizing the perfect, loving obedience that the first Adam never realized, in order to secure eternal life.

Imputation thus refers to the way that Jesus's full obedience, which alone meets the demands for what is required for peace with God, can be counted on his people's behalf. Put differently, imputation describes the legal means by which Jesus's perfect obedience is credited to those who believe in him. Apart from the perfect obedience of Christ, which is imputed by faith alone, we are unable to meet the demands of a holy, just, and perfect God for eternal life.

To understand the nuances of *imputation*, it is helpful to contrast this term with *infusion*. Where righteousness is

Imputation of Righteousness vs. Infusion of Righteousness in Justification: What's the Difference?

Imputation	Infusion
Justification is declarative.	Justification is transformative.
Christ's perfect righteousness is sole ground.	Justification requires believers' obedience.
Righteousness remains Christ's alone.	Christ's righteousness fused with believers' obedience.

imputed, it remains entirely the righteousness of another person. In justification, this means there is no mixing or confusion of Jesus's perfect righteousness with the believer's imperfect righteousness. In contrast, *infused* righteousness refers to the righteousness of the believer being fused together, so to speak, with the righteousness of Christ. On this view, the righteousness in view for justification is both Jesus's righteousness and the believer's renewed righteousness. While this view surely wants to honor the importance of Jesus's work, and even understands believers' obedience to be Christ's righteousness wrought in them,[7] it also necessarily means that to some degree, believers' righteousness becomes part of the foundation for their acceptance before God. In contrast, imputed righteousness remains an *alien* righteousness received by faith alone, which means it does not include the obedience of the believer.

Although there are some ways in which we may legitimately speak of infused righteousness with respect to believers (e.g., in sanctification; see ch. 8), this does not apply to justification.

7. Contrast WLC, question and answer 70. Thanks to Guy Waters for emphasizing this point.

For if justification requires perfect obedience, then our imperfect righteousness will not stand up to scrutiny. Imperfect righteousness, even if sincere, is insufficient for justification. The only righteousness that will suffice is the perfect, entire righteousness of Jesus—his active and passive obedience.

The Importance of Technical Theological Language

For those unfamiliar with theological debates and discussions relating to important doctrines such as justification, the obedience of Christ, imputation, the Trinity, and so forth, the use of such precise, technical terminology may seem like arcane hairsplitting. Yet Christianity is defined by specific doctrines, and these can only be maintained by using carefully defined, technical terms to communicate carefully and accurately biblical truth.

Technical theological terms are necessary to guard and communicate the rich complexities of the Bible. To use terms not found in the Bible to communicate faithfully the contents of the Bible is not only permissible, but is often necessary. We are not limited to only using the terms the Bible uses, for in that case the task would devolve into simply repeating biblical passages. Instead, as it has long been understood in the history of Christianity, specialized, technical terms are necessary to communicate the teaching of the Bible in a consistent, coherent manner.

Imputation is one such word. If we were to confuse imputation of righteousness with the infusion of righteousness in justification, then we would downplay the necessity of Jesus's perfect obedience for justification and misconstrue what God requires for eternal life. This would lead to the conclusion that our works, being less than perfect, are somehow considered as perfect in God's sight, or otherwise sufficient to meet the demands for justification. But this would downplay the necessity of Jesus's perfect obedience and prove inconsistent with God's covenant with Adam in the beginning. Since eternal life requires perfect obedience, we must insist that the obedience that makes us right with God is *only* the obedience of Jesus. Imputation communicates the importance and uniqueness of Christ's perfect obedience. This will also affect how we understand *faith*, as I will argue later.

In this chapter I have discussed some of the key terms related to the obedience of Jesus. Even if someone disagrees with the theology of Jesus's obedience I have introduced (which I will defend further in following chapters), it is important to be clear on what we are discussing, so that we avoid talking past one another.

Looking Ahead

My focus in this chapter has been on definitions. Yet thus far I provided relatively little exegesis. The question ought to arise: Are these definitions consistent with the way that Paul and other New Testament authors speak? Earlier I noted the emphasis that Paul places on the cross. Given this clear emphasis in the New Testament, it is perhaps not surprising that many have disagreed with the notion that Christ's entire righteousness is imputed to believers. This is typically understood as an aversion to the *active* obedience of Christ, whereas the death of Christ (often understood as his passive obedience) seems more biblical to many.

However, as the definitions above indicate, the active obedience of Christ also refers to his death. Likewise, the passive obedience refers to Jesus's life. There is no point in his life where we can separate these two. Given the widespread misunderstanding at this point, it has been necessary to lay out what the terms mean and sketch the most compelling views before discussing the texts themselves.

Now that some key definitions have been clarified, we must turn our attention to whether they correspond to the biblical texts themselves. For this is the real measure of any theological formulation.

EXEGESIS

3

THE OBEDIENCE OF
THE LAST ADAM

I f you travel in the wrong direction from the outset, you'll get lost more quickly. You need to have—and follow—the right directions from the beginning. My home is presently peppered with children's building blocks. When you're making an intricate creation, it's a deflating feeling to get to step 22 and realize you did step 2 incorrectly. To get it right, you often have to start over. The foundation largely determines the final product.

So it is when interpreting Scripture. As we begin considering the biblical basis of the unified obedience of Jesus for salvation, it's important to get the first steps correct. We need to calibrate our interpretive compasses to account for the opening of the Bible, and specifically the role of Adam. In this chapter I want to follow up on the definitions set forth in the previous chapter by looking primarily at two issues.

First, I will look at how Jesus's obedience is portrayed to be the obedience of the second and last Adam in the New Testament. This means it will also be important to consider what was required of the first Adam at the beginning of Scripture.

Second, throughout this chapter I want to show how the obedience of Jesus is not divided, but is viewed as a unity in the New Testament. It is Jesus's entire obedience that saves, which I will discuss more fully in this chapter from Romans 5:12–21.

The Obedience Required of Adam

It's imperative that we start at the beginning. Too often discussions of Jesus's obedience and/or justification begin later in the story, perhaps with Abraham or Israel. But by that point, the wheels are already in motion and the effects of Adam's sin have negatively permeated the world. To understand the contours and necessity of the perfect obedience of Jesus, we have to look at the pattern in the beginning, especially Adam in his original, created state. In this brief section, I will explain how God's requirement to Adam for eternal life was entire, perfect obedience.

It is often thought that Adam was given a limited set of tasks to obey. He was clearly not to eat from the tree of the knowledge of good and evil (Gen. 2:17). He was also, with Eve, to be fruitful and multiply, fill the earth, and subdue it (1:28). Adam was also tasked with serving and guarding the garden of Eden (2:15). But is this all we can say? Was Adam tasked with more than this?

The answer is yes. Adam was required to obey the entire moral law of God.[1] This means he was required to love God entirely. Partial obedience and incomplete love would not suffice.

1. See further Brandon D. Crowe, *The Path of Faith: A Biblical Theology of Covenant and Law*, ESBT (Downers Grove, IL: IVP Academic, 2021), 13–15.

And Scripture makes it clear that love and obedience go hand in hand (e.g., Deut. 5:10; 6:5; 7:9; 11:1; John 14:15, 23). It makes no sense to say that Adam would inherit eternal life if he avoided eating of the tree of the knowledge of good and evil, even if he murdered his children. It would not meet God's requirements if Adam were to serve assiduously in the garden of Eden while also worshiping an idol. Adam was not to be fruitful and multiply by committing adultery. Adam had to be truly, fully obedient, and this obedience was to the moral law of God, which was written on his heart.[2] This means Adam was bound to obey what would later be codified in the Ten Commandments. The Ten Commandments, though given to Israel at a specific moment in biblical history, are nevertheless unique in the way that only they were inscribed upon stone tablets.[3] The Ten Commandments do not focus on the more ceremonial or civil aspects of God's law. Instead, the Ten Commandments summarize the abiding moral law of God, which does not change and which reflects what was required already of Adam in the beginning.[4]

What, then, do we make of the specific prohibition against eating from a certain tree in the garden? The command not to eat from the tree of the knowledge of good and evil was a specific probationary test, but this test summed up all that was required of Adam. Would Adam obey God as Lord, or would he choose his own way? The consequence for Adam's disobedience was death (Gen. 2:17). On the other hand, the blessing for obedience would have been glorious, permanent, eternal life. If Adam passed the test, he would live forever. This is the corollary of the death that would accrue to Adam if he sinned.

---

2. E.g., Turretin, *Inst.*, 9.6.1 (1:604); WCF 4.2.
3. See Sinclair B. Ferguson, *The Whole Christ: Legalism, Antinomianism, and Gospel Assurance—Why the Marrow Controversy Still Matters* (Wheaton: Crossway, 2016), 147–51.
4. See esp. Turretin, *Inst.*, 11.1.22–23 (2:6–7); 11.2.17 (2:12); Bavinck, *RD*, 2:574; see also Irenaeus, *Haer.* 4.15.1; Crowe, *Path of Faith*, 48–50, 55–57.

Charles Hodge on
Adam's Probationary Command

"The specific command to Adam not to eat of a certain tree, was therefore not the only command he was required to obey. It was given simply to be the outward and visible test to determine whether he was willing to obey God in all things."

—Charles Hodge, *Systematic Theology*, 3 vols. (1872–73; repr., Peabody, MA: Hendrickson, 2008), 2:119

Life as the reward for obedience is already conveyed in the account with Adam, but it is further clarified by Scripture's consistent correlation between doing the commandments and life. One important text in this regard is Leviticus 18:5, a text that is echoed many times in Scripture: "You shall therefore keep my statutes and my rules; if a person does them, he shall live by them: I am the LORD." I will return to this text in the next chapter, where we will consider Paul's discussion of it in Galatians 3 (and Jesus's reference to it in Luke 10). Paul's use of this text, in conjunction with Deuteronomy 27:26, attests the principle that eternal life requires complete, entire adherence to the law of God. Although Leviticus 18 is not spoken to Adam per se, it is consistent with what was required of Adam. The pattern of life in tandem with obedience is consistent throughout Scripture. This correlation is realized in the New Testament, where life in the fullest sense comes in accord with Jesus's full obedience to the law of God.

Adam had a goal in front of him. Adam was created sinless (see Eccles. 7:29), but not yet experiencing the fullness of glorious, eternal life. The means of reaching the goal of permanent, glorious life, based on the covenantal arrangement of God, was his perfect obedience. To be clear, this obedience would not *earn* Adam anything. Indeed, it could not. Adam was a created being who was required by nature to obey God. Even perfect obedience would not merit eternal life, strictly speaking. Obedience to their Creator is required of all people. The only reason that Adam's obedience would have yielded eternal life is that God voluntarily condescended (that is, accommodated himself to humanity) and sovereignly set the parameters of a covenant relationship with Adam and promised that he would give glorious life if Adam obeyed fully. Though it is debated whether this administration is best described as a *covenant* with Adam, the basic elements of a covenant are present (covenant parties, stipulations, blessings and curses), and Hosea 6:7 most likely mentions a covenant with Adam.

The covenantal contours of Adam's call to obedience and the reward held out to him provide the proper precedent for understanding Jesus's covenantal obedience in the New Testament.

In sum, it is crucial to understand all that was required of Adam in the beginning. If we think that Adam was only required to do one or a few things, perhaps we will conclude that Christ had to do one or a few things to save us. Though Paul does speak of Jesus's singular act of obedience in Romans 5 (which I discuss below), it is misguided to think that Adam was only required to do *one* act of obedience. Adam was not merely prohibited from one act; he was required positively to love and obey God, and this requirement was focused in a particular way in the probationary test. Where Adam failed, Jesus as the last Adam succeeded.

This is not just a construct of systematic theology; this is a point made explicit by the apostle Paul more than once. To overcome the first Adam's disobedience requires the full obedience of the last Adam.

Paul on Adam, Christ, and Obedience unto Life

We turn now to the teaching of the apostle Paul about the relationship of Jesus to Adam in Romans 5. There can be no doubt that the cross is the climactic act of Jesus's obedience and is central for Paul's understanding of the work of Christ and justification. And yet the way that Paul relates the obedience of Christ to the disobedience of Adam encourages us to see that the cross of Christ is not an isolated act of obedience, but is an integrated—if climactic—aspect of Jesus's unified, entire obedience.

The Argument of Romans 5:12–21

One of the most important passages for understanding the obedience of Jesus is the Adam-Christ comparison Paul makes in Romans 5:12–21. A great deal of theology is packed into this passage, and we must tease out its implications carefully. Simply put, here Paul speaks of the sin of one man, Adam, which led to death and condemnation for all (5:12, 18). In contrast, the obedience of one man, Jesus Christ, leads to justification and life for all (5:18). Through the disobedience of Adam the many were constituted (*katestathēsan*) sinners; through the obedience of Jesus Christ the many will be constituted righteous (5:19).[5]

Despite a number of tricky issues in these verses, Paul is primarily concerned in 5:12–21 to explain parallels between Adam and Christ. Adam's one sin led to death for all people because, in some sense, "all sinned" (5:12). This passage starts with and sustains an emphasis on the tragedy of the sin of Adam that

5. Many modern versions translate *kathistēmi* as "made righteous," but this verse speaks more about one's *status* than about moral transformation per se. See Thomas R. Schreiner, *Romans*, 2nd ed., BECNT (Grand Rapids: Baker Academic, 2018), 293. For reasons why this is important, see the distinctions between justification and sanctification that I discuss in chs. 8–9. See also the discussion of John Murray, *Redemption Accomplished and Applied* (Grand Rapids: Eerdmans, 1955), 122–25.

led to the reign of death over all. Paul makes this point, explicitly or implicitly, no less than eight times in these ten verses. Likewise, at least six times Paul explicitly or implicitly relates righteousness or justification to life. For example, on the one hand, in 5:12 Paul states that sin entered the world through one man, and death entered through sin. On the other hand, in the conclusion of this section Paul proclaims that whereas sin reigned in death, grace reigns in righteousness unto eternal life (5:21). For Paul, righteousness leads to life (5:18).

Central to Paul's argument are the real actions of two representative men: Adam and Christ. Adam's sin brought the tragic reality of condemnation and death to all because he acted as a representative. The answer to Adam's sin is the obedience of a second representative man, Jesus Christ, which leads to righteousness and life. The two key figures in world history concerning condemnation and justification are Adam, the progenitor of death, and Christ, the progenitor of life.

Romans 5 and the Integrated Obedience of Jesus

How, then, does Paul's overarching point about sin and death, righteousness and life relate to the perfect, unified obedience of Jesus (active and passive)? The key comes in 5:18–19, which reads:

> Therefore, as one trespass led to condemnation for all men, so one act of righteousness leads to justification and life for all men. For as by the one man's disobedience the many were [constituted] sinners, so by the one man's obedience the many will be [constituted] righteous.[6]

These verses speak to at least three issues pertaining to the obedience of Jesus. First, the obedience of Jesus that leads to

6. Modified from the ESV.

eternal life is not an isolated act, but is Jesus's entire obedience. Second, Paul's argument requires that perfect obedience is necessary for eternal life. Third, Jesus is the representative last Adam whose full obedience leads to a better result than Adam's sin. These points all require more comment, after which I will respond to some possible objections.

1. The obedience of Christ in Romans 5:18–19 is most likely not limited to Jesus's obedience on the cross, but entails Jesus's *entire* obedience. In 5:18 Adam's trespass (*paraptōmatos*) is parallel to the righteous act of Christ (*dikaiōmatos*). Echoing the use of the same term in 5:16, where *dikaiōma* is often translated "justification," Christ's righteous act in 5:18 refers to his perfect obedience, which provides the foundation for justification. In 5:19 it is through the disobedience of one man (Adam) that the many were made sinners. This parallels the way the many will be made righteous—through the obedience of one man (Jesus Christ).

Yet in this passage the righteous act (Rom. 5:18) and obedience of Christ (5:19) are singular. From this, many have concluded that Christ's one act of righteousness, and his one act of obedience, in 5:18–19 is Jesus's obedience in death. Certainly the cross is central to Paul, and he even speaks a few verses earlier of being saved by Jesus's death: "For if while we were enemies, we were reconciled to God through the death of his Son, much more surely, having been reconciled, will we be saved by his life" (5:10). Yet in Romans 5:10 Paul speaks not only of reconciliation by the death of Christ but also of being saved by Jesus's (resurrection) life (see also 8:33–34). Similarly, in 4:25 Paul speaks of Jesus being handed over for our trespasses and raised for our justification. Again, the death *and* resurrection of Christ are in view.

This is significant because the resurrection of Christ is the vindication of Jesus's entire, perfect obedience (see 1 Tim.

3:16). The resurrection is not *only* the vindication of Jesus's death (though it was that); Jesus's deliverance from death was a demonstration and declaration that sin had no claim on him. He was sinless, which means he always did what was required (which is more extensive than only *avoiding* certain things). The resurrection therefore assumes his perfect obedience throughout his life. Instead of trying to decipher which singular act of Christ Paul has in view in Romans 5:18 (as though any one action could be siphoned off or isolated from others), we should recognize that the singular righteous act more likely refers to the entire obedience of Jesus, which culminates in his death.

Moreover, even if Paul does have Jesus's death primarily in view, his overall argument necessitates that Jesus's death incorporates, sums up, and completes the obedience of Jesus's entire, substitutionary life.[7] Paul's argument in Romans 5:12–21 shows that eternal life requires complete righteousness.

2. Paul's argument in Romans 5:12–21 shows that complete righteousness is necessary for eternal life. This is the requirement that must be met in justification. We must correlate the obedience of Jesus that brings justification and secures eternal life (5:18–19, 21) to the biblical emphasis that justification and the right to eternal life can only be a reality where the covenantal requirements of perfect obedience have been met.

Adam was presented with the prospect of the curse of death if he chose the path of disobedience (Gen. 2:17; see also Rom. 6:23), whereas the blessing of (glorious, eternal) life was held out to Adam if he obeyed. This reality is underscored in Romans 5:12–21 by the link between sin, condemnation, and death that came through Adam on the one hand, and righteousness, justification, and (eternal) life that come through Christ on the other hand.

7. Echoing the language of Bavinck, *RD*, 3:378.

Justification addresses the problem of sin. Sin is any transgression of the law of God, whether by commission or omission. As Paul states earlier in Romans, not only have all sinned (3:12–18, 23), but there is no one who is righteous, does good, or seeks God (3:10–12). Later Paul states that the wages of sin is death (6:23), but he also draws attention to the positive side—the principle that life comes by keeping the commands—when he quotes Leviticus 18:5 ("if a person does them [the commandments], he shall live by them") in Romans 10:5.[8]

Justification must account for both aspects of sinfulness (i.e., sins of commission and omission). Therefore, the obedience of Christ that provides the answer to the sin, condemnation, and death of Adam is a full-orbed, perfect, unified obedience. Anything less than perfect obedience would not lead to justification and eternal life.

3. Jesus is the representative last Adam whose obedience leads to a better result than Adam's trespass. Adam is the representative for all humanity who do not trust in Christ. Christ is the representative for all those who look to him by faith for salvation. Adam's representative trespass led to condemnation and death; Christ's representative obedience leads to justification and life.

The gift of justification is therefore possible because of Christ's role as a new Adam. And the gift of life is better than the trespass (Rom. 5:15–16). Eternal life is forfeited by only one transgression (Rom. 6:23; see also James 2:10), whereas eternal life is not gained simply by one righteous deed.[9] To be viewed as righteous, we must have met the demands of the law entirely and perfectly. The logic of imputation, explained in chapter 2, is built on this two-Adam structure. Adam's representative sin is reckoned legally—that is, imputed—to all humanity. In a simi-

8. I will say more about Lev. 18:5 in ch. 4.
9. Turretin, *Inst.*, 1.4 (1:9–16).

lar but better way, Christ's representative obedience is imputed to all who are united to him by faith. This means that although only Christ is perfectly obedient, that obedience is reckoned to all those who are united to him by faith.

Possible Objections

I have argued that Romans teaches not that Christ's death alone leads to justification and life, but that justification depends on Jesus's entire, integrated obedience. However, a number of objections might be lodged at this point. Here I interact with three of the weightiest.

Objection 1: Christ's death is the one act of obedience

First, it may be objected that Paul's contrast between Adam and Christ focuses on *one* act of each man: Adam's eating the forbidden fruit and Christ's death on the cross. Focusing on one act of Adam and one act of Jesus seems to reflect some early Christian traditions where the sin of Adam in relation to a tree is contrasted with Christ's obedience on a tree. The second-century church father Irenaeus averred, "So, by means of the obedience by which He obeyed unto death, hanging upon the tree, He undid the old disobedience occasioned by the tree."[10] This approach seems to reflect Paul's tendency to emphasize the cross and the passage's focus on the specific sin of Adam. This would be particularly fitting if Paul speaks in Romans 5:18 of "one trespass" (*henos paraptōmatos*) and "one act of obedience" (*henos dikaiōmatos*).

Despite the points in favor of such an argument, this objection is not decisive for several reasons. To begin, it's not entirely clear from the syntax that "one" (*henos*) refers to one "trespass"

---

10. Irenaeus, *Epid.* 34. Translation from Irenaeus, *On the Apostolic Preaching*, trans. John Behr, PPS (Crestwood, NY: St. Vladimir's Seminary Press, 1997), 62. See also Irenaeus, *Haer.* 5.16.3.

(*paraptōmatos*) and one "righteous act" (*dikaiōmatos*) in Romans 5:18. Though this is quite possible, given Paul's focus on two, key individuals throughout this passage (i.e., Adam and Christ), it is better to take "one" (*henos*) as a reference to one *man* in each instance in 5:18. This would yield the translations "trespass of one man" and "righteous act of one man," emphasizing the representative roles of each man—Adam and Christ. This option better accords with the context in which *henos* ("one") consistently refers to one *man* (5:12, 15–17, 19). Thus, the emphasis throughout the passage is not on the identification of the specific act of each man, but on the representative role of each man.

Further, even if Paul does have the death of Christ *largely* in view in 5:18–19 (and it is quite possible that he does), his logic that Jesus's righteous act yields justification necessitates that more than *only* the death of Christ is in view.[11] Justification requires full righteousness; it cannot be gained by one act.[12] In this light, even if we take "one" (*henos*) adjectivally to refer to *one* trespass and *one* act of righteousness in 5:18, this one act of righteousness could be construed as the *entire* obedience (singular!) of Jesus. Since Jesus's obedience cannot be divided, it would be fitting to speak summarily of *one* act of righteousness.

Christ's obedience is better than Adam's disobedience because it was not simply one isolated act of obedience, but was a lifelong obedience that overcame the curse of sin. Thus, the righteous act and obedience of Christ in Romans 5:18–19—even *if* Paul speaks of *one act* of righteousness—must refer to Jesus's obedience as a "compact unity."[13] To return to Irenaeus, although he does compare Jesus's obedience on the tree

---

11. See Robert Letham, *The Work of Christ*, CCT (Downers Grove, IL: InterVarsity, 1993), 131–32.

12. Turretin, *Inst.*, 9.9.39 (1:626).

13. John Murray, *The Epistle to the Romans*, 2 vols., NICNT (Grand Rapids: Eerdmans, 1959–65), 1:201.

to Adam's disobedience centering upon a tree, Irenaeus has a much more comprehensive schema (i.e., *recapitulation*) in which Jesus's *lifelong* obedience is necessary to overcome the sin of Adam.[14] So it is with Romans 5:18–19: inasmuch as the death of Christ may be in view, this act of obedience cannot be separated from Jesus's unified, lifelong obedience.

One additional point is necessary: even if one were to limit the obedience of Christ in Romans 5 to his death, this would not be the same as saying Romans 5 has only the *passive* obedience of Christ in view since the passive obedience of Christ describes his lifelong obedience. Likewise, the active obedience of Christ extends throughout his life (and culminates in his death). So even if Paul's focus in Romans 5 is on Christ's death, it would therefore necessarily still be on *both* the passive obedience and active obedience of Christ; these are logical (rather than temporal) distinctions pertaining to his unified obedience. Put starkly, the death of Christ on the cross is integral to his active obedience (see, e.g., Matt. 26:39; Mark 14:36; Luke 22:42; John 4:34).

As it pertains to justification, I have argued that we can correlate the forgiveness of sins (and certainly the problem of sin is in view in Rom. 5:12–21, and also in 5:8–11) to the passive obedience of Christ, and the right to eternal life (which is explicitly emphasized in 5:17–21) flows from the active obedience of Christ. Inasmuch as both the forgiveness of sins and the right to eternal life are in view, in a passage that expounds the obedience of Jesus as a representative figure, we are on firm ground to conclude that the dual aspects of Christ's obedience must be in view in Romans 5:12–21.

Objection 2: The law does not require perfect obedience

A second objection is that Paul does not say that *perfect* obedience is necessary for eternal life. This objection typically

14. See, e.g., Irenaeus, *Haer.* 3.18.1; 3.18.6–7; 3.21.10; 3.23.1; 4.4.2; 4.8.2; 5.1.2; 5.21.1.

assumes the obedience required of the *Mosaic law* as a covenant administration. But when speaking about Adam, justification, and the obedience of Christ, we must not begin with the Mosaic law; we must start with the law given to Adam long before Moses.

Further, to address the level of obedience required by the law requires us to be sensitive to the various ways that *law* (Greek: *nomos*) is used in Scripture, including in Paul's Letters. We must define our terms clearly. There can be no doubt that Paul quite often means the Mosaic law when he uses the term *nomos*. This is the way that he uses the term in Romans 5:20. Yet Paul also has a role for the moral law of God in a way that precedes and transcends the Mosaic administration of the law. Paul's use of Leviticus 18:5 may point in this direction (Rom. 10:5; Gal. 3:12), as does his use of *nomos* in Romans 7:21, and possibly 6:14.[15]

This broader theology of law must be kept in mind when Paul discusses the obedience of Christ in contrast to the disobedience of Adam. What did Adam disobey if the law came *after* his trespass (5:20)? It could not have been the Mosaic law. It must have been the moral law of God. Likewise, though Jesus obeyed the law of Moses, as the second and last Adam he obeyed the moral law of God completely and perfectly, which was originally written on Adam's heart.

This is why it is so important to consider Romans 5 carefully and (following Paul's lead) to include Adam in conversations pertaining to justification. If eternal life is contingent upon perfect obedience, according to God's covenantal requirements, then two men must dominate the conversation: the first Adam and the last Adam. For many who deny that the "law" requires perfection, the discussion focuses on what the Mosaic law requires, and the discussion likely starts with Abraham or Israel.

15. E.g., Turretin, *Inst.*, 11.1.3 (2:1); Schreiner, *Romans*, 375.

However, to start with either Israel or Abraham and to focus entirely on the law of Moses is to miss the foundational beginning in Genesis 1–3, which lays the groundwork for Paul's theology of salvation. When we start with Adam—as Paul does in Romans 5—it becomes clearer that the Mosaic law is not the first law in Scripture, and we can see with greater clarity why so many in the history of interpretation have maintained that perfect obedience is necessary for eternal life. Perfect obedience was required in the beginning, and it remains necessary for eternal life even after sin has entered the world. This helps us understand why Christ's full obedience as Mediator was necessary for salvation.

Objection 3: Adam is an illustration, not a historical person

Third, it may be objected that Paul's point in Romans 5:12–21 need not rely on a historic person called Adam to be theologically valid. It is said that Paul is using an example from the Bible to illustrate a truth, and his argument does not hang on whether or not Adam was the first person, or even a real person. Therefore, it is said that we should be cautious about making too strict a historical connection between Christ's obedience and Adam's disobedience. So runs the objection.

Though this comparatively novel theological position has become increasingly popular in recent years, it reflects a flawed reading of Paul's argument, and it collapses under the weight of insuperable theological objections. Paul does not invoke Adam simply to *illustrate* his point. Adam is more than an illustration for Paul. In Romans 5 Adam is understood as a historical person whose past actions explain the origin and universality of sin and death that affect everyone. Adam's real actions can only be overcome by the real work of Christ. Paul's argument thus necessitates that Adam was really the first person. To conclude instead that Adam was not historical is to unhinge Paul's entire argument.

Not only in Romans 5 but also in 1 Corinthians 15 Paul's argument requires that Adam was a real person. In fact, in two key texts in which Paul explains the saving work of Christ (Rom. 5; 1 Cor. 15), he explains the reality of Christ's work in relation to the reality of Adam. If Adam is not the progenitor of the human race, Paul's explanation for the unity of the entire human race's sinfulness and the universality of death is wrong. Likewise, if Adam is not the first man, then Paul's explanation of the nature of Christ's work as the head of the new humanity leading to justification does not stand. Adam's real existence, as the first human being, must be a nonnegotiable for those who hold fast to Paul's exposition of the gospel.

This view that Adam was a real person is not limited to Paul, but is assumed throughout Scripture (including Gen. 1–3; 5:1–3; 1 Chron. 1:1; Hosea 6:7; Matt. 19:4; Mark 10:6; Luke 3:38; Jude 14). Those who hold to the sufficiency, authority, and clarity of Scripture must reckon with the manifold, clear references to Adam in Scripture. Though there are many complex debates on the origins of humanity, the Bible sets forth a clearly articulated position with respect to the reality and representative role of Adam. Scripture beckons us to believe its testimony that Adam was really the first man. This is important for a discussion of Jesus's obedience because Paul portrays Jesus as a new Adam whose obedience realizes and overcomes what Adam failed to do. This framework explains why Jesus had to be perfectly obedient and how Jesus's perfect obedience can be applied representatively to others.

Some may object that, though he was a *real* person, Adam was not necessarily the *first* person. However, the polarity of options Paul sets forth in Romans 5:12–21 and 1 Corinthians 15:21–28, 44–49 allows for no other person who is not made in either the image of the first man, or the image of the second man. Paul gives two options, and those two options cover all of humanity: all who are not represented by Christ (the second man) are represented by Adam (the first man). Further, Christ's work only applies to those who are naturally in Adam; Paul's logic requires that for someone to be saved by Christ, they must first be in Adam. Paul does not leave open a third option that some people may have existed prior to, or somehow apart from, Adam. Denying Adam was the *first* person also fails to account for the universal tragedy of death, which is not natural, but only entered because of the specific sin of Adam.[16]

Romans 5 teaches that the entire obedience of Jesus—in both its active and passive dimensions—is necessary for eternal life. This is consistent with the covenantal conditions originally given to Adam. If we *only* received forgiveness of sins, then we would not have met the requirements of eternal life, and the justification in view in 5:17–21 would not be full justification. Instead, Paul's glorious doctrine of justification is built upon Jesus's *entire* obedience as its necessary foundation.

The Obedience of Jesus in Romans 5 in the History of Interpretation

Given the importance of Romans 5, it will be helpful to pause and listen to a few other voices from church history. Perhaps my interpretation sounds novel, perhaps not. Either way, it's important to recognize that the interpretation I have argued for is commonly reflected in the history of interpretation. I want to illustrate this from three sources. The first voice is the second-century apologetic writing the *Epistle to Diognetus*. The second voice is that of John Calvin in his discussion of Romans 5:19 in his *Institutes of the Christian Religion* and in his commentary on Romans. The third voice is from a work of systematic theology of the seventeenth century—Francis Turretin's *Institutes of Elenctic Theology*.

16. See further Richard B. Gaffin Jr., *No Adam, No Gospel: Adam and the History of Redemption* (Phillipsburg, NJ: P&R, 2015), 12.

1. The Righteousness of the Son in the Epistle to Diognetus[17]

The *Epistle to Diognetus* provides an important window into early Christian theology. In chapters 7–9 the author discusses Christology and salvation. The preexistent Son was active in planning and accomplishing redemption (*Diogn.* 9.1–6). In 9.2–3, 5b the Son's righteousness covers sins. Here a positive work of salvation is attributed to the Son's righteousness. It appears that the author finds the answer to humanity's (plurality of) unrighteous deeds in the (singular) righteousness of the Son.

This possibility is further supported by one of the more interesting passages in *Diognetus*: "O the sweet exchange, O the incomprehensible work of God, O the unexpected blessings, that the sinfulness of many should be hidden in one righteous person, while the righteousness of one should justify many sinners!" (9.5a).[18] This "sweet exchange" points to the entirety of the life of the Son given in exchange for unrighteous sinners, who are themselves unable to attain eternal life (9.1, 3–4). It is the Son's righteousness that enables humanity to attain God's kingdom, life, and justification (9.1, 4). In short, in *Diognetus* the "sweet exchange" is best viewed as the entirety of the work of the Son in the incarnation, both extending to a positive accomplishment of righteousness and serving as a sacrificial ransom in his death.

Further, this argument from *Diognetus* 9 appears to echo language from Paul's Letters, and Romans 5:18–19 in particular. Most noteworthy are the contrasts between the *one* and the *many* and between *disobedience* and *righteousness*. In *Diognetus* 9.5b the righteousness of one man overcomes the lawless-

17. This section is taken from Brandon D. Crowe, "Oh Sweet Exchange! The Soteriological Significance of the Incarnation in the *Epistle to Diognetus*," ZNW 102 (2011): 96–109. Used with permission from Walter de Gruyter.

18. Translation from Michael W. Holmes, ed., *The Apostolic Fathers: Greek Texts and English Translations*, 3rd ed. (Grand Rapids: Baker Academic, 2007), 711.

ness of humanity, and this righteousness includes the entire scope of his redemptive life. This seems to take the "righteous act" and "obedience" of Jesus in Romans 5:18–19 to refer to the entire, singular, unified obedience of Jesus.

To summarize, *Diognetus* echoes Pauline language and concepts and draws upon language from Romans 5 to communicate the wide-ranging obedience of Jesus that qualifies believers for eternal life. This is especially communicated by the language of "exchange."

2. John Calvin on the Obedience of Christ in Romans 5:19

Moving ahead in the history of interpretation, we should also appreciate the balance of John Calvin's discussions of Romans 5:19. In his *Institutes of the Christian Religion*, Calvin addresses the need for Jesus's entire obedience to save us. I introduced this quote in the previous chapter, but it's instructive to look at the quote in broader context:

> How has Christ abolished sin, banished the separation between us and God, and acquired righteousness to render God favorable and kindly toward us? To this we can in general reply that he has achieved this for us by the whole course of his obedience. This is proved by Paul's testimony: "As by one man's disobedience many were made sinners, so by one man's obedience we are made righteous" [Rom. 5:19]. In another passage, to be sure, Paul extends the basis of the pardon that frees us from the curse of the law to the whole life of Christ: "But when the fullness of time came, God sent forth his Son, born of woman, subject to the law, to redeem those who were under the law" [Gal. 4:4–5]. . . . In short, from the time when he took on the form of a servant, he began to pay the price of liberation in order to redeem us.[19]

19. John Calvin, *Institutes of the Christian Religion*, ed. John T. McNeill, trans. Ford Lewis Battles, 2 vols., LCC 20–21 (Philadelphia: Westminster, 1960), 2.16.5 (1:507).

To be sure, Calvin also recognizes that often Scripture attributes our salvation to the death of Christ. However, this does not negate the necessity of the lifelong obedience of Christ for salvation. Indeed, even in Christ's death "his willing obedience is the important thing because a sacrifice not offered voluntarily would not have furthered righteousness."[20]

Likewise, in his commentary on Romans Calvin emphasizes the perfect righteousness of Christ as that which alone meets the divine requirements for justification:

> As [Paul] declares that we are made righteous through the obedience of Christ, we hence conclude that Christ, in satisfying the Father, has provided a righteousness for us. It then follows, that righteousness is in Christ, and that it is to be received by us as what peculiarly belongs to him. He at the same time shows what sort of righteousness it is, by calling it obedience. And here let us especially observe what we must bring into God's presence, if we seek to be justified by works, even obedience to the law, not just in this or that part, but in every respect perfect. . . . Away then with those who confidently lay claim to the righteousness of works, which cannot otherwise exist than when there is a full and complete observance of the law; and it is certain that this is nowhere to be found.[21]

For Calvin, Romans 5:18–19 teaches us that only perfect obedience suffices for justification. Further, notice Calvin's emphasis that perfect obedience belongs to Christ alone. This means that if this obedience is to be counted for us, it does not become our obedience. It always remains Christ's obedience. This is why it is necessary to guard the term *imputation* of righteousness—in order to preserve the perfection and uniqueness of Christ's work.

20. Calvin, *Institutes*, 2.16.5 (1:508).
21. John Calvin, *Commentaries on the Epistle of Paul the Apostle to the Romans*, trans. John Owen (repr., Grand Rapids: Baker, 2003), 212–13.

3. Francis Turretin on the Obedience of Christ in Romans 5

Francis Turretin (1623–87) discusses the obedience of Christ in Romans 5 in a way that is characteristically careful and thorough.[22] Turretin provides several arguments why it is insufficient to say that the death of Christ is the only act of obedience in view in Romans 5:19. As he discusses the mediatorial office of Christ and the nature of Christ's satisfaction, Turretin explains that the obedience of the Mediator includes both active and passive dimensions. Turretin then adduces various texts to defend the notion that Christ's satisfaction entails the obedience of his life (and not just his death).

He begins this defense from Romans 5:19, and his argument features several spokes. First, in this passage Paul treats the whole obedience of Christ without limitation, which means that it must refer to the obedience of Christ from the beginning to the end of his life, and this must not in any way be incomplete or imperfect.

Second, the obedience of Romans 5:19 has in view not only obedience to the sanction of punishment but principally to keeping the law's commandments.

Third, the gift of righteousness which Paul speaks of here cannot be predicated of the sufferings of Christ.

Fourth, Paul has in view an obedience that is opposed to the disobedience of Adam. Since Adam was required to obey the whole law, the obedience in view must be the obedience to the whole law.

Fifth, Paul addresses here what was due from us, regarding both "punishment and precept."[23] In other words, the righteousness in view in Romans 5:19 is not only one act of righteousness, but must be the righteousness that arises from a fullness of obedience.

---

22. The comments in this section closely follow Turretin, *Inst.*, 14.13.17 (2:450).
23. Turretin, *Inst.*, 14.13.17 (2:450).

Turretin concludes, "If by one sin guilt came upon all, righteousness does not pass from one act upon all because evil is from any kind of defect, but good requires a perfect cause."[24] Turretin later adds that the righteousness of Christ is not divided. Thus, even if Scripture ascribes redemption to Jesus's blood and death, this cannot be to the exclusion of the obedience of his life of humiliation. In Turretin's words:

> If our salvation and redemption are ascribed to the blood and death of Christ, this is not done to the exclusion of the obedience of his life because nowhere is such a restriction found. Elsewhere . . . it is extended to the whole obedience and righteousness of Christ. Rather it must be understood by a synecdoche by which what belongs to the whole is ascribed to the better part because it was the last degree of his humiliation, the crown and completion of his obedience (which supposes all the other parts and without which they would have been useless).[25]

Thus the *entire* obedience of Jesus is necessary for eternal life, and therefore the entire obedience of Jesus must be in view in Romans 5.

Conclusion

Many more voices from the history of interpretation could be invoked to support the argument that Paul views the obedience of Christ in its entirety to be necessary for justification and eternal life. Additionally, many other texts from Paul's Epistles that speak about the righteousness of Christ could be invoked, such as 1 Corinthians 1:30 and 2 Corinthians 5:21. Elsewhere Paul states that justification in Christ is not based on any work of

24. Turretin, *Inst.*, 14.13.17 (2:450).
25. Turretin, *Inst.*, 14.13.23 (2:452). A *synecdoche* employs a part to represent the whole.

our own (Titus 3:5–7). In Ephesians Paul's Adam Christology (see 1:10, 20–22) is tied to his theology of salvation, whereby the work of Christ alone saves (2:8–9). In Galatians the cross is clearly important (2:19–20; 3:10–14), though elsewhere Paul seems to have in view a more thoroughgoing obedience beyond only the cross (3:22–4:5).[26]

To understand the work of Christ, we have to start at the beginning. Much hinges on what was required of Adam. If Adam was required to do only one act, then this could be taken to support the notion that the obedience of Jesus that saves us is his death. But if Adam was required to love and obey God fully, then it is much more likely that the *entire* obedience of Jesus is necessary for eternal life.

It is the entire obedience of Jesus that meets the requirements for eternal life. It is not proper to divide this obedience into parts, as though some aspects were more necessary than others. The death of Christ is not isolated from his life, but is the crowning achievement of his entire incarnate obedience. Paul's emphasis on the death of Christ in many passages is fitting for one whose unified obedience is always both active and passive. Both these aspects of Christ's obedience are highlighted by emphasizing the climactic act of his obedience unto death. Consistent with what I argued in the previous chapter, in Romans 5:12–21 Paul teaches that justification consists in both the forgiveness of sins and the right to eternal life.

For Paul, it is the entire, perfect obedience of Christ that provides the ground for justification. Nothing less will suffice.

---

26. Richard N. Longenecker, "The Obedience of Christ in the Theology of the Early Church," in *Reconciliation and Hope: New Testament Essays on Atonement and Eschatology Presented to L. L. Morris on His 60th Birthday*, ed. Robert Banks (Grand Rapids: Eerdmans, 1974), 145–46 and 146n1.

4

THE MOSAIC LAW AND PERFECT OBEDIENCE

I s a tomato a fruit or a vegetable? Even if you know the right answer, you still might hesitate before answering. This seems like a trick question. On the one hand, the tomato is technically a fruit in the scientific sense—its seeds are within it. On the other hand, practically speaking the tomato is often classified with vegetables. Though technically a fruit, tomatoes are often listed among vegetables at restaurants.

Which is it? The way you answer that may depend on your framework. You could make an argument that a tomato could be categorized both as a fruit and as a vegetable, depending on the angle from which you look at it. Either way, your answer may require further explanation.

In this chapter I address a question that is similar to the tomato question: Did the law of Moses require perfect obedience? As with many "gotcha" questions, the answer to this question requires further explanation. Asking this question leads us into some of the most difficult and complicated areas of New Testament interpretation. Thin answers will not suffice; we must answer with nuance.

In the previous chapter I argued that Adam was required to be perfectly obedient to meet the covenantal commands for eternal life. In this chapter I will argue that the law of Moses is multifaceted. On the one hand, as a covenant administration it did not require perfect obedience for the faithfulness of God's people. One could walk righteously in faith even apart from one's own perfect obedience. At the same time, the law of Moses attests the principle of life on the basis of obedience, which New Testament authors highlight to challenge our proclivity to rely on our own, incomplete obedience. So you could make the argument that, depending on one's perspective, the law of Moses both does and doesn't require perfect obedience.

This perspective is clearest in Paul's Letters, so I'll devote the bulk of space in this chapter to Paul's arguments in Romans, Galatians, and Philippians. I will also show how Paul's teaching accords with Jesus's teaching, particularly in Luke 10. Both Paul and Jesus attest the reality that if one seeks life by obedience to God's commands, then that must be perfect obedience. This way of life is contrasted with the way of faith, which trusts in another's work for salvation. That other's work is the perfect obedience of Jesus.

One caveat is necessary here: the issues relating to the law of Moses are exceedingly complex and would require many books to explore thoroughly. It is not my intent to address this complexity in depth. My aim is much more modest. In this chapter I want to provide a handle on the complexity by focusing on the key question throughout this study: Does the Mosaic law affirm that perfect obedience is necessary for eternal life? I will argue that it does.

The Mosaic Law in Redemptive History

When it comes to what God requires of his people, the law of Moses is central. The law of Moses is found succinctly in Exodus 20–23, but is also diffused throughout the books of Exodus, Leviticus, Numbers, and Deuteronomy. The law of Moses was given to Israel as a redeemed people after their redemption from Egypt and governed Israel as a nation. This law of Moses is typically what the New Testament authors mean when they speak of *law*.

It's important to recognize several features of this law. First, the law of Moses is not the first law in Scripture. Even before the law of Moses was given, people knew what God required, and they were culpable for their sin. For example, Abraham is described as obeying God's voice, charge, commandments, statutes, and laws (Gen. 26:5), even though the law of Moses had not yet been given. And even earlier than this, the flood wiped out most of humanity because people were culpable for their sin (6:5). This trajectory can be traced all the way back to Adam—to his being tasked with obeying the moral law of God entirely. If we start our questions about the law and obedience with the law of Moses, then we will miss the necessary, prior foundation in Adam.

Second, the Mosaic law was given *after* Israel was redeemed from Egypt in the exodus. It was not given to them as a "ladder of good works" that they had to climb to inherit eternal life. Redemption and the law were gifts of God (Deut. 4:1–8), and eternal life was in the Old Testament by faith no less than in the New Testament. Abraham and Moses are both used as examples of faith in the New Testament (e.g., Rom. 4:3; Gal. 3:6; Heb. 11:8–19, 23–29; James 2:23; see also Gen. 15:6).

These people of faith from the Old Testament were looking ahead to a heavenly inheritance; they did not receive in their lifetime the fulfillment of what was promised to them. By faith, they looked forward to eternal life, but not on the basis of their own works. Jesus picks up on the name of God revealed to Moses in Exodus 3:6 ("I am the God of your father, the God of Abraham, the God of Isaac, and the God of Jacob") to speak of the reality of eternal life from the Old Testament—God is not the God of the dead, but of the living. The Sadducees, who denied the reality of resurrection life, erred by understanding neither the Scriptures nor the power of God (Matt. 22:29–32; Mark 12:24–27; Luke 20:37–38).

Third, after Adam's sin, perfect obedience was not necessary for Old Testament believers in order to walk in covenant faithfulness with God on a day-to-day basis. Otherwise, no one who lived under the law of Moses could have pleased God, for every person we meet in the Old Testament—and every person in world history born naturally since Adam—is a sinner. But we know that God provides a way for his people to walk before him and be blameless (Gen. 6:9; 17:1; Deut. 18:13), even though they are sinners. This is the path of true faith and repentance, which is also the way of walking according to God's commands. Yet this did not require *perfect* obedience, practically speaking, for God's people. The word of God was not too hard for them to keep (Deut. 30:11–14). Yet tragically, God's people all-too-willingly went astray.

Fourth, the law of Moses as a *comprehensive* rule for life was only temporary. This is why Paul says in the New Testament that Christ is the end, or goal, of the law (Rom. 10:4—on which see below), and this explains Paul's argument in Galatians 3–4 as he shows the foolishness of trying to go back in time in redemptive history, as though life would be better if we could revert to the era when the Mosaic law was the governing principle. A similar point is made in Hebrews. The Mosaic law as the governing covenant administration was temporary.

Yet here again we need nuance, for the New Testament writers do not simply dismiss the law of Moses. Indeed, the New

Testament writers continue to draw attention to the moral law of God within the Old Testament. Think here especially of the Ten Commandments. Paul continues to affirm the command to honor one's father and mother, and even recognizes that it is the first command with a promise (Eph. 6:1–3). To fulfill the law means loving one another (Rom. 13:8–10). Jesus similarly states that the law requires love for God and love for neighbor (Matt. 22:37–40; Mark 12:29–31; Luke 10:27), which is a fitting summary of the Ten Commandments and the entire law of Moses. Only the Ten Commandments were written on stone, highlighting both their importance and permanence. In contrast, some other portions of the law of Moses dealt more with the sacrificial system and worship and with legal matters pertaining particularly to the nation of Israel. The Ten Commandments continue into the New Testament era, while the sacrificial system and civil aspects of God's law proved to be temporary. This is why Christian theology has so often distinguished between ceremonial, civil, and moral aspects of God's law. Indeed, already in the Old Testament a distinction is understood between ritual and true obedience. Thus the prophets often lament the hollow offering of sacrifices from offerers whose hearts are far from God (e.g., 1 Sam. 15:22; Ps. 40:6–8; Isa. 1:11; Jer. 4:4, 14; 7:1–34; Hosea 6:6).

While a sharp line cannot always be drawn between these three "divisions" of God's law, the point is that some aspects of the Mosaic law were temporary, and some are permanent. The permanent can be correlated to the moral law of God, which was already binding on people even before the Mosaic law was given.[1] The moral aspects of the law are abiding, and they remind us that God grants eternal life on the basis of perfect obedience to this law. Indeed, the Mosaic law speaks

---

1. This does not mean that there were no moral aspects to the civil and ceremonial aspects of God's law, for indeed these teach us much about loving God and neighbor.

to this when it highlights the principle that life comes on the basis of law keeping.

A key text is Leviticus 18:5: "You shall therefore keep my statutes and my rules; if a person does them, he shall live by them: I am the LORD." Paul quotes this text in Romans 10 and Galatians 3, and Jesus probably alludes to it in Luke 10. This passage provides a case study in the need for nuance. For on the one hand, Leviticus 18 is part of a law that requires God's people to obey his commands, but also recognizes inherent sinfulness and provides ways of atoning for sin and a means to fellowship with God (i.e., by means of the sacrificial system and the faith of its participants). On the other hand, the New Testament uses this text to point to the abiding reality that life, in the fullest sense, comes by keeping the law of God, in the fullest sense. Put simply, Leviticus 18:5 both is given to a redeemed people *and* attests the principle that eternal life requires perfect obedience. We will see below that Leviticus 18:5 is invoked in Galatians, Romans, and the Gospels in ways that highlight the need for Jesus's perfect obedience.

To summarize: On the one hand, the law given through Moses in its redemptive-historical administration did not require perfect obedience for sinful covenant members to walk in faithfulness in daily fellowship with the Lord. Indeed, it was not possible for them to be perfectly obedient since they were born naturally after Adam. On the other hand, Paul found in the Mosaic law the principle that fullness of life necessarily goes hand in hand with perfect obedience. So, while the Mosaic law as part of the covenant of grace (i.e., as part of God's gracious plan of salvation) did not require nor expect perfect obedience for a redeemed people on a daily basis, the moral law of God more fundamentally does require perfect obedience for inheriting salvation (and thus for justification). Put differently: Though faithful Israelites under the Mosaic administration of the law could please and obey God by faith, perfect obedience was ultimately required for them to inherit eternal life. Their justification, just like the justification of believers in the New Testament era, is grounded on the perfect obedience of Christ.

To show how this is the case, we must turn to the New Testament.

The Mosaic Law and Perfect Obedience in Paul's Letters

Galatians 3

Galatians is one of the most important books for understanding Paul's teaching about how we are made right with God (i.e., justification). If justification requires perfect obedience, then we might expect to find this alluded to in Galatians. I believe that we do. But this issue requires us to consider one of the most debated passages in the New Testament: Galatians 3:10–14. The Mosaic law attests the principle that perfect obedience is necessary for justification, and thus for eternal life. Galatians 3:10–14 reads:

> For all who rely on works of the law are under a curse; for it is written, "Cursed be everyone who does not abide by all things written in the Book of the Law, and do them" [Deut. 27:26]. Now it is evident that no one is justified before God by the law, for "The righteous shall live by faith" [Hab. 2:4]. But the law is not of faith, rather "The one who does them shall live by them" [Lev. 18:5]. Christ redeemed us from the curse of the law by becoming a curse for us—for it is written, "Cursed is everyone who is hanged on a tree" [Deut. 21:23]—so that in Christ Jesus the blessing of Abraham might come to the Gentiles, so that we might receive the promised Spirit through faith.

In this passage Paul contrasts the way of faith with the way of works. Just prior to this (3:1–9), Abraham is set forth as a model of the righteousness that comes by faith (Gal. 3:6; see

Gen. 15:6), which is consistent with Abraham as the model of faith elsewhere in the New Testament (e.g., Rom. 4:1–5).

Galatians 3:10 (and Deuteronomy 27:26)

Paul's discussion of Abraham in Galatians 3:1–9 provides necessary context for interpreting 3:10–14. A key question comes in 3:10—who are the people that are cursed? Many modern translations render the opening phrase as something like "all who rely on [the] works of the law." This translation of those who "rely on" works of the law interprets the Greek phrasing (*hosoi . . . ex ergōn nomou eisin*), which might more simply be translated "all those who are [in some way] characterized by works of the law."

So how should we translate this verse? And what group of people is in view? This has been widely debated. A prominent traditional position, which is reflected in many modern translations (such as the ESV above), is that Galatians 3:10 refers to all who rely on a legalistic standing before God on the basis of their own works. Such people are under a curse. The reason for this interpretation is based in large measure on Paul's appeal to Deuteronomy 27:26 in Galatians 3:10: "Cursed be everyone who does not abide by all things written in the Book of the Law, and do them." This apparently all-encompassing statement, seen in the need to do *all* that the law requires, assumes it is necessary for a person to keep the entire law to avoid the curse of God. Thus, perfect obedience is required.

The logic of this interpretation is as follows:

A. All who rely on works of the law for justification are under a curse.

B. [Implied:] No one (whether Jew or gentile) is able to obey the law perfectly.

C. Therefore, every person stands naturally under a curse before God.

This interpretation, the "implied premise" view, is the preference of well-known interpreters such as Martin Luther and John Calvin. Calvin observes simply, "All who have transgressed any part of the law are cursed."[2] The curse therefore applies universally to both Jews and gentiles. Perhaps the most glaring drawback to this view, however, is the ambiguity of the Greek phrasing. The text does not explicitly say that *all people* are under a curse; this conclusion must be inferred. Additionally, this point assumes that the law of Moses in some sense required perfect obedience. Yet we have already seen that the law of Moses did not set forth an unrealistic level of obedience for God's people.

Because of such difficulties, many instead object to the notion that Galatians 3:10 is about those who *rely on* works of the law. Instead, it refers to the Jewish people, who were distinguished from other nations by distinctive, covenantal works such as circumcision, dietary laws, and Sabbath observance. On this view, the curse of the law in 3:10 refers to the climactic curse of exile that applied particularly to Israel for violating the law of Moses. Those under a curse are therefore not humanity in general, but specifically God's covenant people.

We could call this the "corporate-exilic view."[3] This view takes seriously the Old Testament context of Deuteronomy 27, which is spoken to God's people before they enter the promised land and warns them about exile that would result from disobedience. It also appreciates the role of the law given to Israel in redemptive history.

2. John Calvin, *Commentaries on the Epistles of Paul to the Galatians and Ephesians*, trans. William Pringle (Grand Rapids: Baker, 2003), 89; see also Calvin, *Institutes of the Christian Religion*, ed. John T. McNeill, trans. Ford Lewis Battles, 2 vols., LCC 20–21 (Philadelphia: Westminster, 1960), 2.7.5 (1:353–54). For Luther see *LW*, 26:248–68. Luther and Calvin are just the tip of the iceberg for this view.

3. See, e.g., the view of N. T. Wright in *The Climax of the Covenant: Christ and the Law in Pauline Theology* (Minneapolis: Fortress, 1992), 144–48.

However, despite some strong arguments in favor of this corporate emphasis, this view does not best represent Paul's argument. It is better to understand Galatians 3:10 and the quotation of Deuteronomy 27:26 to refer to any person who relies on works for his or her standing before God. Paul teaches that perfect obedience is necessary and that no one can meet the demand. This more traditional reading best captures Paul's logic for several reasons.

First, Paul contrasts faith and works in this passage, and Abraham serves as a model of faith in Galatians 3:6–9. This makes it unlikely that Paul uses the language of *curse* in 3:10 to refer to *true* believers (that is, true children of Abraham) among God's people who underwent the curse of exile.[4] Instead, the curse applies to those characterized by works in contrast to faith. If the curse in 3:10 were only for the Jewish people defined by the Mosaic law, it would mean Paul characterizes Abraham's true children as people of works. Yet Paul explicitly states right before this that Abraham's true children are people of faith (3:7)—like Abraham himself (3:6, 9). Moisés Silva captures the crux of the issue: "It is implausible that Paul would indiscriminately describe his fellow-Jews as people not characterized by faith."[5] The true offspring of Abraham have always been those of faith (3:7), and such people are not best understood as remaining under a curse. That being said, *all people*—whether Jews or gentiles—who are not characterized by faith (but by works of the law) are under a curse.

Second, it is not a problem for the "implied premise" position that Paul does not explicitly say that no one obeys the law

4. Francis Turretin says explicitly that this curse cannot apply to believers—even those who lived in the old economy. See *Inst.*, 12.10.29 (2:255–56); 17.2.13 (2:697–98).

5. Moisés Silva, "Abraham, Faith, and Works: Paul's Use of Scripture in Galatians 3:6–14," *WTJ* 63 (2001): 260; see also Herman Ridderbos, *Paul: An Outline of His Theology*, trans. John Richard De Witt (Grand Rapids: Eerdmans, 1975), 154.

perfectly in Galatians 3:10. This point is only implied, but it is consistent with Paul's argument throughout Galatians, where Paul often leaves his logic unstated, requiring the reader to fill in the gaps.[6] Indeed, it is not only the "implied premise" position that fills in gaps in Paul's logic. If one understands with the "corporate-exilic" view that the curse in 3:10 is the curse of corporate exile, that also would fill in a perceived gap in Paul's logic since Paul does not mention the exile explicitly.[7]

The context of Galatians helps. In this portion of Galatians Paul is contrasting faith and works. It would be puzzling for Paul to say that Abraham's true offspring are people of faith (3:7, 9) *while also saying* they are characterized by works of the law in 3:10. Instead, true believers are people of faith, and Paul contrasts people of faith with those who are characterized by the works of the law. Additionally, elsewhere Paul clearly views *all humanity* to be under the law (Rom. 2:12–16; 6:14–15),[8] and all people as sinners, subject to death and the wrath of God (see 3:5, 9, 23; 5:12–13; Gal. 3:22). This universal emphasis, which includes both Jew and gentile, best accords with the universal scope of the curse in Galatians 3:10. Paul's universal focus is also apparent in his emphasis on "everyone" and "all" in his quotation of Deuteronomy 27:26.[9] This also attests the abiding principle that full-orbed law keeping is necessary to yield full-orbed life.

Third, the "implied premise" position, which assumes that no sinner has kept the law perfectly, follows a long and weighty exegetical tradition. It was not only the view of Luther and Calvin, but is evident at least as early as the second-century church father Justin Martyr (*Dial. 95*).

6. Silva, "Abraham, Faith, and Works," 253–54; Craig S. Keener, *Galatians: A Commentary* (Grand Rapids: Baker Academic, 2019), 235–36.
7. Silva, "Abraham, Faith, and Works," 257, 261–62.
8. The example of Rom. 6 comes from Douglas J. Moo, *Galatians*, BECNT (Grand Rapids: Baker Academic, 2013), 267.
9. Compare Turretin, *Inst.*, 9.4.8 (1:598); HC, question and answer 10.

In sum, Galatians 3:10 is best taken as a reference to any person (whether Jew or gentile) who is not characterized by the faith of Abraham and is therefore not justified before God by faith. Paul's logic demands that perfect obedience is necessary if one wants to be accepted before God on the basis of law keeping—a point he makes clearer in the following verses.

Galatians 3:11 (and Habakkuk 2:4)

One's interpretation of Galatians 3:10 sets the stage for the following verses. That Paul views perfect obedience to the law to be necessary for justification is clarified in 3:11, where he specifically speaks of justification by faith. Quoting Habakkuk 2:4, Paul writes that the righteous person will live by faith, since it is clear that no one is justified by the law. This continues Paul's contrast between faith and works, and it echoes the language from Galatians 2:16 to speak of justification by faith, and not by works of the law.

This approach to the *believer's* faith as the focus of Habakkuk 2:4 in Galatians 3:11 has been challenged in recent decades. Instead, some have argued that "the righteous one will live by faith" is a reference to Jesus himself. This would yield the translation "the righteous one [Jesus Christ] will live by his faithfulness." (A similar reference to Jesus's own faithfulness is frequently identified in Galatians 2:16.) While this approach to Galatians 3:11 is possible, it is unlikely that Habakkuk 2:4 refers to Jesus's own faithfulness. Habakkuk 2:4 recalls Abraham's faith in Genesis 15:6; Abraham did not live by his faithfulness, but by faith in God's provision.[10] Paul's focus in Galatians 2–3 is not on Christ's *faithfulness*, but on our *faith in Christ*. This coheres best with the plenteous, explicit statements about *faith in Christ* throughout the New Testament (see, e.g., Acts 9:42;

---

10. See further Moisés Silva, *Interpreting Galatians: Explorations in Exegetical Method*, 2nd ed. (Grand Rapids: Baker Academic, 2001), 165–67.

10:43; 11:17; 14:23; 16:31; 18:8; 22:19; see also 11:21; 13:39), and in Paul's Letters specifically (e.g., Gal. 2:16; Eph. 1:13; Phil. 1:29; 1 Tim. 1:16; 3:16).[11]

Galatians 3:12 (and Leviticus 18:5)

Paul thus emphasizes the impossibility of being justified on the basis of law keeping in contrast to faith. This is the point of his quotation of Leviticus 18:5 in Galatians 3:12. This verse also raises many questions. For example, why does Paul say that the law is not of faith? And why does he seem to pit one Old Testament passage (Hab. 2:4) against another Old Testament passage (Lev. 18:5)?

In short, Paul quotes Leviticus 18:5 to invoke a principle from the law of Moses that to be justified before God on the basis of law keeping requires entire, perfect obedience.[12] This is contrasted with being justified by faith. Galatians 3:12 is the second half of a contrast between two ways of living. One way of living, seen in 3:11, is by faith (like Abraham). The second way of living is by works of the law, illustrated by Leviticus 18:5. This continues Paul's contrast between faith and works.

In Galatians 3:12 Paul employs Leviticus 18:5 to show why perfect obedience is necessary for eternal life. If one were to live *fully* by works of the law, it would require full obedience. When combined with the all-encompassing description of doing *all* the things written in the book of the law (Deut. 27:26 in Gal. 3:10; see also Gal. 5:3), Paul highlights the incessant *doing* that

11. See also Moisés Silva, "Faith Versus Works of the Law in Galatians," in *The Paradoxes of Paul*, vol. 2 of *Justification and Variegated Nomism*, ed. D. A. Carson, Peter T. O'Brien, and Mark A. Seifrid, WUNT 2/181 (repr., Grand Rapids: Baker Academic, 2004), 227–34.

12. On Lev. 18:5, see Turretin, *Inst.*, 8.3.7 (1:575–76); 8.6.4 (1:583); 11.23.2 (2:141); 12.2.3 (2:174); 12.3.6 (2:186); 12.7.32 (2:227); 12.12.14–22 (2:565–68); 14.13.20 (2:451); Bavinck, *RD*, 2:565; 3:174, 183–84, 225–26; 4:184–85; Geerhardus Vos, *Reformed Dogmatics*, ed. and trans. Richard B. Gaffin Jr., 5 vols. (Bellingham, WA: Lexham, 2012–16), 2:41; 3:132–34; Ridderbos, *Paul*, 156.

must be characteristic of anyone who seeks eternal life by law keeping. That *eternal* life is in view in Leviticus 18:5 is clear from the role the promised land had in typifying eternal life[13] and the use of "life" throughout Galatians (2:19–20; 5:25; 6:8).[14]

Paul invokes Leviticus 18:5 to prove that eternal life requires perfect obedience. This is the light in which to read Paul's contrast between the two ways of living. To walk the path of works for justification would require that path to be walked perfectly, something manifestly impossible for sinners. To walk by faith means to trust in the one who has borne the curse for us (Gal. 3:13), which assumes that Christ himself is the one who walked the path of obedience perfectly (see also 4:4–5). Justification by faith in Christ means trusting in the perfection of Christ himself, and not in our own, imperfect works.

This interpretation of Leviticus 18:5, however, has been questioned as being out of accord with Paul's thought and anachronistic in a first-century setting. It is objected that Leviticus 18:5 can't be teaching that perfect obedience is necessary, for it was given to a redeemed people for whom perfection was not required. It is argued that this reading of Leviticus 18:5 seems to turn the Mosaic law on its head, as if the Mosaic covenant was given as a means to earn one's salvation. This view notes that it was common in first-century Judaism (which provides important context for Paul's thought) to view the Mosaic law as a gracious covenant. If so, then it sounds as if Leviticus 18:5 has often been hijacked as a prooftext extracted from its original context. These objections could also be applied to Deuteronomy 27:26, which is said to be not about perfect obedience, but about sufficient obedience to inherit the promised land.

I appreciate the force of these objections and the value that these fresher interpretations propose to offer. We must take

13. Turretin, *Inst.*, 8.6.4 (1:583); 12.7.32 (2:227).
14. Keener, *Galatians*, 248–49, 552–53.

historical and Old Testament contexts seriously, and we must understand the Mosaic covenant positively. Yet I don't think the traditional reading is anachronistic, nor do I believe that newer interpretations are more compelling. Too many problems remain. Instead, it is best to understand Paul as viewing the Mosaic law through two lenses. In what follows, I discuss the nuances of the Mosaic law in Galatians 3:12 a bit further.

1. *Paul's argument about law reliance and justification.* Let's start with Paul's argument in Galatians. While it is true that the Mosaic law was never about working one's way to God, this is precisely the point that Paul has to make clear to his readers. For it seems that many were—if not in explicit word, at least in deed—holding that one could be acceptable to God based on what one has done (see Gal. 3:11).

Paul counters this by showing how law reliance for acceptance with God—to any degree—runs counter to the faith that characterizes Abraham and his true children. Abraham could not have been righteous based on works of the Mosaic law, since the law came 430 years later (Gal. 3:17). Instead, Abraham was justified before God by faith (see 3:6–9).

It is true that the Mosaic law was given to a redeemed people and was God's beneficent condescension to his people. But sinful people have the resolute tendency to twist good gifts of God for improper ends. This appears to have been happening in Galatia. Paul's argument, drawing on the law itself, shows the foolishness of clinging to and claiming law keeping as the means for justification.

2. *Tensions in the Old Testament?* Any cogent interpretation of Galatians 3:10–14 has to wrestle with why there is apparent tension in Paul's use of the Old Testament. He seems to use the Old Testament positively with respect to Habakkuk 2:4 (3:11) and more negatively with respect to Deuteronomy 27:26 (3:10)

and Leviticus 18:5 (3:11). On the one hand, the law is gracious and calls for faith. On the other hand, the law is not of faith. How can both be true? This is "an exceedingly complex problem."[15]

The interpretation I am setting forth, which focuses on the inability of humanity perfectly to obey the law, provides the best answers to the apparent tensions in Paul's use of the Old Testament, and to apparent tensions in the Mosaic law. It may be helpful to understand the Mosaic law like a tomato; it can be understood from two angles. On the one hand, the Mosaic law was given to a redeemed people and did not unrealistically require perfection for faithful living in the day-to-day. The Mosaic law was an administration of the covenant of grace. This means that the law of Moses is a redemptive, gospel message. Just as a tomato is most essentially a fruit, the law of Moses is most essentially a gracious covenant. At the same time, just as a tomato can function as a vegetable as well, the law of Moses attests the principle that perfect obedience is necessary to yield justification and eternal life. Like a tomato, it can be understood from more than one angle.

In Galatians 3 Paul shows that the law of Moses attests the principle of Leviticus 18:5 ("do this and live"), which underscores the people's inability and weakness, showing them that their own righteousness is insufficient fully to meet the demands of the law. He draws attention to this principle even though the law itself is *essentially* a gospel message.[16] In other words, Paul uses Leviticus 18:5 not to speak of the Mosaic covenant as a whole, "but strictly as taken for the moral law abstractly and apart from the promises of grace."[17]

3. *Leviticus and the Mosaic law in redemptive history.* Paul's two ways of speaking about the Mosaic law require us to parse

15. Ridderbos, *Paul*, 153.
16. Compare Turretin, *Inst.*, 12.7.32 (2:227), with 12.7.43 (2:230).
17. Turretin, *Inst.*, 12.12.21 (2:267–68).

out carefully the various dimensions of the Mosaic law. This is something that Paul's opponents had not done. They apparently appreciated neither the strictness of the law's demands nor the role of the law in preparing for the coming of Christ. But Paul also explains in Galatians how the law as a covenant administration was given until the promised seed came (Gal. 3:19). As such, it was a temporary administration, which exacerbated the problem of sin (see 3:22–24). The false teachers in Galatia had a defective and truncated understanding of the coming of Christ in relation to the Mosaic law. They misunderstood the provisional character of the Mosaic law, even as they underestimated the degree of obedience that is necessary for someone to rely on law keeping as a means of acceptance before God.

In this light, when Paul says that the law is not of faith in Galatians 3:12, he is saying (as he does in 3:23) that the law belongs to the era of anticipation. Christ is the substance of our faith, who has appeared in the fullness of time, bringing a new era of salvation history—the age of freedom and fullness of blessing (3:24–28). To rely on works of the law now that Christ has come is not only to misunderstand the entire obedience that is necessary for justification. It's also to belong to the old order of things, which fails to do justice to Christ as the object of our faith. To cling to the old order is to make Christ of no value (5:2) and to turn one's back on God's appointed means of justification (3:11).

4. *Leviticus and the perfect obedience of Jesus.* Leviticus 18:5 not only highlights our sinfulness; it also brings us back to Adam. Leviticus 18:5 (and Deut. 27:26) captures succinctly the principle given to Adam in the beginning—that eternal life is tethered to perfect obedience.[18] That requirement has not

---

18. Turretin, *Inst.*, 8.6.4 (1:583).

been abrogated after the sin of Adam. By his obedience as the representative last Adam, Jesus meets the requirement for eternal life.

In sum, the conclusion that perfect law keeping is ultimately necessary for true justification makes sense of all of Paul's statements we have seen thus far in Galatians 3:10–12. Paul uses both Deuteronomy 27:26 and Leviticus 18:5 to show the strict standard of perfect obedience that is required for eternal life, and this is contrasted with the way of faith in Christ—the one who met the demand of perfect obedience.

Galatians 3:13-14 (and Deuteronomy 21:23)

In Galatians 3:13 we at last come to *explicit* mention of Christ himself: Christ redeemed us from the curse of the law by becoming a curse for us. The "us" in 3:13 must be the same group in view in 3:10 who are subject to a curse. That means the "us" for whom Christ bore the curse in 3:13 refers to *all* true believers (whether Jew or gentile). The curse is not simply the curse of exile, but is the more all-encompassing curse of God's wrath on humanity due to sin. Christ bore the curse as a curse for all true believers on the cross (see Deut. 21:23). Yet for Paul, the death of Christ was not the final word. Jesus bore our curse as the perfect substitute. The definitive proof of this is his resurrection from the dead, demonstrating that sin had no claim on Jesus.

I explore this topic more fully in chapter 7, but it is noteworthy that Paul's sermon in Acts 13 sheds helpful light on Galatians 3. In his sermon at Pisidian Antioch, which was in Southern Galatia (which was also probably the location of his audience in the letter of Galatians), Paul emphasizes the resurrection of Jesus (see Acts 13:30). The resurrection was the answer to Jesus's unjust death, and in Acts 13:29 Paul probably alludes to Deuteronomy 21:23 (the same verse quoted in Gal. 3:13). As the risen Lord of all, Jesus reigns over an everlasting kingdom, and it is through this man that Paul proclaims forgiveness and justification (Acts 13:37–39). Reading Galatians 3 and Acts 13 together further supports the view that forgiveness and justification are based on the perfect obedience of Jesus, which is demonstrated by his resurrection.

Conclusion: Galatians

In Galatians 3:10–14 Paul demonstrates that justification is by faith for all who believe, apart from any human works (including those focused on the law of Moses). No one can keep the law perfectly, which is why we need a substitute to bear the curse for us.

Galatians presents us with two options: justification by works of the law or justification by faith. To be justified by the law, perfect obedience is necessary. To attempt, as did Paul's adversaries, to require circumcision for salvation would be to teach that justification, in some sense, takes imperfect works into account. Such an approach, however, can only lead to bondage. True freedom and justification come through faith in Christ—who redeemed us from the curse of the law.

Romans 10

Romans 10 exhibits an argument similar to Galatians 3. Paul has great grief for his own people, who have the law but have often missed its purpose. Many have not understood God's righteousness in Christ, but have sought their own righteousness (Rom. 10:1–3). The end, or goal, of the law is Christ, through whom comes righteousness for all who believe (10:4).[19] To miss Christ is to miss the goal of the law; it is also to misunderstand the righteousness required by the law.

---

19. Romans 10:4 is "one of the most controverted passages in Pauline literature" (Thomas R. Schreiner, *Romans*, 2nd ed., BECNT [Grand Rapids: Baker Academic, 2018], 531). Along with Schreiner (*Romans*, 531–34), I believe *telos* most likely means both "goal" and the "end" of the law as a covenant administration.

This last point is evident from Paul's use of Leviticus 18:5 in Romans 10:5 ("For Moses writes about the righteousness that is based on the law, that the person who does the commandments shall live by them"). In contrast to the righteousness that comes by faith is the righteousness that is characterized by the law. As in Galatians 3:12, Paul must mean here the law as a principle, abstracted from its redemptive message and its relation to Christ (which many had missed; see Rom. 10:4). To return to the tomato analogy: Paul knows the Mosaic law is fundamentally gracious (just as a tomato is fundamentally a fruit), but here he focuses on the strict-obedience principle attested in the Mosaic law (which may be compared to the way a tomato often *functions* as a vegetable). The law as a *principle of works* is opposed to faith, for if pursued consistently, the law requires entire obedience if one seeks life by the strictness of the law's demands.

In contrast, the righteousness of faith looks to Christ as the means to meet God's demands. In Romans 10:5–13 Paul contrasts our inability to achieve righteousness by means of the law with the righteousness that comes by faith. Whereas the law apart from faith requires perfect "doing" for eternal life, the righteousness characterized by faith looks to the work of Christ. We need not ascend into heaven or plumb the depths of the earth (10:6–7). We are not "being asked to bring about an incarnation or a resurrection."[20] We are not required to be perfect, for Paul has already made it clear that this is impossible after the fall of Adam (see 3:23; 5:12–21). Instead of seeking a righteousness that comes by means of law keeping (see 9:32), we instead look to Christ, the goal of the law, who has done what we could not do. In his incarnation Jesus has met the demands of the law, which is demonstrated by his resurrection from the dead (10:9; see also 4:25; 5:18–19).

20. See Joseph A. Fitzmyer, *Romans: A New Translation with Introduction and Commentary*, AB 33 (New Haven: Yale University Press, 1993), 590.

For Paul, it is not faith as a generic principle that is superior to works. Instead, it is faith in Christ, the one who fulfills the law and grants us forgiveness of sins and eternal life, which we could not attain on our own. All who call on the name of the Lord Jesus—the glorious one, resurrected from the dead—are saved (10:13).

Philippians 3

In Philippians 3, as well, Paul contrasts the righteousness that comes by means of the law with the righteousness that comes by means of faith in Christ. Here Paul speaks of his former life, in which he trusted in works of the flesh (3:4). Paul even states that he was blameless with respect to the righteousness of the law (3:6). But if the law required perfection, as I have argued, how could Paul be blameless with respect to the law? Was he claiming that he was perfect? If not, does this verse undermine the view that the law of Moses required perfection?

This passage has engendered much debate. But in brief, the best view is that Paul speaks in Philippians 3:6 of his former *perception* of his righteousness according to the law. Paul viewed himself as blameless. But his zeal was not according to the knowledge of the truth (Rom. 10:2). For like the countrymen for whom he agonizes in Romans 10, Paul formerly was unaware of true righteousness, which comes through faith in Christ as the goal of the law. Paul's former confidence was in his flesh, not in God (Phil. 3:4).

In contrast to the boast of Paul's flesh, he came to realize that all his deeds were nothing compared to knowing Christ. The righteousness he has found in Christ comes not by means of the law, but through faith in Christ. Paul no longer places his trust in his own works—however we would define those works—but in the righteousness that comes through faith in Christ. Whereas Paul earlier may have counted his actions under the law to his advantage apart from Christ (Phil. 3:7), Paul later came to reject the notion that any of his works could render him acceptable before God (3:7–8). This makes best sense of Paul's language of *confidence in the flesh* in 3:3–4 (see also 2 Cor. 3:4; Eph. 3:12).

In Philippians 3:9 Paul contrasts "the righteousness from the law" (*dikaiosynēn tēn ek nomou*) with the righteousness of God (*tēn ek theou dikaiosynēn*), which comes through faith in Christ (*dia pisteōs Christou*). "The righteousness of God" has been widely debated, but it is best to understand it as the righteousness that comes from God and is consistent with his own character of judging justly. This God-given righteousness is contrasted with a righteousness that relies on a person's own works. Only the righteousness that comes from God through faith in Christ suffices before God.[21]

Paul had come to recognize that even his most zealous works did not elicit eternal life. Life comes through faith in Christ, the one who has been raised from the dead, vindicating his life of perfect obedience (see Phil. 2:6–11). By faith in Christ Paul attains eternal, resurrection life. Paul contrasts the life of faith to the path of trusting in one's own works. When Paul counts his own works rubbish in order to gain Christ (3:8) and to be found in him, having a righteousness that comes from God (3:9), this most likely refers to the imputation of Christ's righteousness.[22]

Conclusion: Paul's Letters

The best way to make sense of the tensions in Paul's statements with respect to the Mosaic law is to understand the law through two lenses. First, the law is a positive, redemptive administration of the covenant of grace that sets forth the way of faith. This is apparent in much of what Paul says about the law, including the use of Deuteronomy 30:14 in Romans 10:8: "The word is near you, in your mouth and in your heart." This

21. See Ridderbos, *Paul*, 163–64; Turretin, *Inst.*, 16.2.15 (2:643).

22. G. K. Beale, *A New Testament Biblical Theology: The Unfolding of the Old Testament in the New* (Grand Rapids: Baker Academic, 2011), 473.

is from the same context in Deuteronomy where Moses says that the word is not too hard for Israel to do (Deut. 30:11). Paul clearly understands the law of Moses positively.

So when Paul says that the law is not of faith, he must be speaking of the law from a vantage that does not appreciate the true intent of the law. The law should point us to Christ and the righteousness that comes by faith. Seeking righteousness on the basis of law keeping requires one to keep the law perfectly. But this is an impossibility after the sin of Adam. To place our faith in Christ is to place our faith in the one who has overcome the sin of Adam and kept the law of God perfectly. Our faith must be in Jesus, the one who has descended from heaven and risen from the dead. In him is life, not in our own, imperfect works—however sincere they may be.

Jesus's Comments on Perfect Obedience to the Law

Parable of the Good Samaritan (Luke 10:25–37)

In the Gospels Jesus speaks of perfect obedience to the law in a way that coheres quite well with Paul's statements about the law. Jesus affirms the law of Moses in many ways, including his emphasis on the two great commandments: loving God and loving one's neighbor.[23] In Luke this is found in the context of the parable of the good Samaritan (Luke 10:25–37). A lawyer tested Jesus: "Teacher, what shall I do to inherit eternal life?" (10:25). When Jesus countered by asking the lawyer how he read the law, the lawyer responded with the two great commands (10:27). Jesus affirmed this interpretation of the law, and then answered the lawyer's original question: "Do this, and you will live" (10:28), which almost certainly is a reference to Leviticus 18:5.

23. Here I am following Brandon D. Crowe, *The Last Adam: A Theology of the Obedient Life of Jesus in the Gospels* (Grand Rapids: Baker Academic, 2017), 178–82.

We must wrestle with what Jesus means by this statement. Did Jesus really mean that eternal life comes by loving God and loving one's neighbor? Or was he speaking hypothetically to further the conversation? The best answer is to see Jesus doing something similar to Paul. Jesus was both challenging the lawyer's righteousness (and, by extension, all readers' righteousness) and assuming the principle that eternal life and keeping the commandments are correlated.

The parable strongly emphasizes "doing" (*poiēsas*), which (in addition to Jesus's challenge in Luke 10:28) frames the entire episode (10:25, 37).[24] It is also clear that the lawyer's understanding of his ability to keep the two great commands was insufficient. Though his answer was correct (10:27–28), in practice the lawyer's perspective on whom he was required to love was insufficient. It is also important to recognize that the lawyer desired to justify himself (10:29). Jesus's parable shows the radical demands of God's law. Though the principle of "do this and live" is true, Jesus's challenge indicates that neither the lawyer nor anyone else fully meets these demands. That Jesus concludes the parable with "Go, and do [*poiei*] likewise" (10:37) does not undermine this interpretation, for we are still bound to keep the law, even if we cannot keep it perfectly.

It is also assumed in Luke 10, as it is in Paul's Letters, that Jesus uniquely was able to "do this and live." I will discuss the obedience of Jesus in the Gospels further in chapter 5, but it is obvious that the Gospels present Jesus as fully obedient. In this light, it's interesting that the lawyer's question about inheriting eternal life is basically the same as asking, "What must I do to participate in the resurrection of the righteous?"[25] If so, then the question seems indirectly to shed light on the rationale for

24. Klyne R. Snodgrass, *Stories with Intent: A Comprehensive Guide to the Parables of Jesus* (Grand Rapids: Eerdmans, 2008), 349.
25. Darrell L. Bock, *Luke*, 2 vols., BECNT (Grand Rapids: Baker, 1994–96), 2:1023.

Christ's own resurrection. The lawyer's powerlessness to secure resurrection life by law obedience serves as a foil to Christ himself, whose resurrection proved that he was able to "do this and live." Jesus's perfect obedience led to resurrection life.

Rich Young Ruler (Matthew 19:16–22; Mark 10:17–22; Luke 18:18–23)

The parable of the good Samaritan leads us to a similar encounter with the rich young ruler. Like the lawyer in Luke 10, the young ruler asks Jesus what he must do to inherit eternal life (Matt. 19:16; Mark 10:17; Luke 18:18). Jesus responds by challenging the man's degree of obedience, stating baldly in Matthew, "If you would enter life, keep the commandments" (19:17). Jesus then recounts the so-called second table of the Ten Commandments, which the lawyer affirms he has kept. Despite the lawyer's protestations of his obedience, Jesus's final challenge reveals the man's true heart and lack of sufficient obedience to meet the requirements for eternal life (see Matt. 19:21–22; Mark 10:21–22; Luke 18:22–23). The rich young ruler did not love his neighbor as he ought (see esp. Matt. 19:19), and he refused Jesus's demand to give generously to those in need. This greediness was probably also a violation of the commandment not to steal (Matt. 19:18 and parallels in Mark 10:19; Luke 18:20).

Jesus's challenge to the rich young ruler shows the heights of what the law of God requires. The young man's refusal to part with his possessions revealed a heart that was not fully committed to God, which means he also broke the first commandment. It is instructive that in Matthew Jesus urges the man to be perfect (*teleios* [19:21]), which recalls the perfection of God's loving character in Matthew 5:48. Matthew's account, therefore, rather clearly links the commands Jesus gives to the rich young man to the need to love as God loves. Whereas the rich young ruler was unable to meet these demands, Jesus himself can offer eternal life (see Matt. 19:29 and parallels in Mark 10:30; Luke 18:30), which presupposes Jesus's unique ability to do that which is required for life.

In both of these encounters, Jesus challenges would-be followers with the demands of God's law. If they were to inherit eternal life by their own actions, then perfect obedience would be required. This principle is found in the Mosaic law, even though that law calls for faith. Jesus and Paul agree that there are two paths to life: a path of works, which requires entire conformity to God's law, and a path of faith, which rests on the works of another for life. The only way to inherit eternal life is to trust in the works of another, for our works cannot be perfect enough to merit eternal life.

Conclusion

The main question I am addressing in this book is whether perfect obedience is necessary for eternal life. This question requires us to consider the graciousness of the law of Moses, but also the principle it attests that eternal life is contingent upon perfect obedience. Does the Mosaic law teach the principle that perfect obedience is necessary for salvation? According to Paul and Jesus, the answer is yes.

We also must relate the Mosaic law to the law given to Adam, recognizing that only in the estate of humanity before the fall would perfect obedience have been possible. Since Adam represented all humanity, no natural person after him can achieve perfection. All are born sinners—all except for Jesus, who was not represented by Adam, but is instead the head of a new humanity. Only Jesus realizes the perfect obedience necessary for eternal life.

5

JESUS'S OBEDIENCE AND SALVATION IN THE GOSPELS

When you're used to something, you may not notice it. How many residents of Rome daily pass by the Coliseum or Forum without giving them a second glance? How many Parisians drive down the Champs-Élysées more focused on the traffic than the Arc de Triomphe? How many Londoners cross the Thames without looking twice at the Palace of Westminster or Westminster Abbey, just a stone's throw away? Yet tourists will travel from all over the world to see these sights.

Familiarity often breeds indifference.

This can also be true when it comes to the obedience of Jesus in the Gospels. In the previous chapter I argued that Jesus, like Paul, uses the law of Moses to challenge those who trust in their own works for salvation. No natural person is able fully to live on the basis of personal obedience. But Jesus does more than only talk about perfect obedience; he also lives it. The tension between his challenges to others and the stringency required by the law is resolved in the perfect obedience of his own life. Few would disagree that the Gospels present Jesus as the fully obedient Son of God. But how does this relate to his accomplishment of salvation? In what sense was his obedience necessary? Were all aspects of his obedience necessary? What is the logic by which the obedience of Jesus benefits his people? How does his obedience save his people from their sins (see Matt. 1:21)?

In this chapter I will focus on some ways that the Gospels present Jesus as a representative, whose actions benefit his people.[1] Jesus's obedience is the obedience of an anointed representative. Important texts for this interpretive approach are found in Jesus's baptism and temptation, which are closely related to his work of binding the strong man. The Gospel writers highlight several ways that Jesus's obedience is necessary for salvation, including the way Jesus's obedience fulfills Scripture in the Gospel of Matthew and the various "it is necessary" statements in the Gospel of Luke. Jesus also teaches us much about what the law of God requires, and this is to be understood in light of what he himself does. The Gospels view the obedience of Jesus's life and death as a unity, so that both aspects are necessary for salvation.

In addition, we will look at how the Gospel of John speaks of Jesus as the obedient Son of God and the proper response of faith. John's perspective complements the other Gospels and helps us see more explicitly our need to abide in Christ.

In short, much as we saw in the previous chapter, the way of life is the way of faith in Jesus. Only Jesus is sufficiently obedient to meet the requirement for eternal life.

1. Portions of this chapter build upon Brandon D. Crowe, *The Last Adam: A Theology of the Obedient Life of Jesus in the Gospels* (Grand Rapids: Baker Academic, 2017).

Jesus as Obedient Representative

In chapter 3 I noted that Paul's argument in Romans 5 builds on two key figures in world history: Adam and Christ. The perfect obedience of Jesus is contrasted with the disobedience of Adam. Both men are representatives whose actions affect others. The Gospels provide us with a similar perspective—Jesus is a unique individual who begins a new humanity. He is the true Israelite, living the life that an Israelite should have lived. More than that, he is the true human, living the life that God requires of humanity. And because he is a representative—the king of Israel, but also the second and last Adam—his perfect obedience benefits his people.

We see this already with Jesus's unique birth. Though Paul does not mention the virgin birth explicitly, his argument in Romans 5 necessitates that Jesus was not represented by Adam's actions. Yet Paul also teaches us that anyone who would save humanity from sin must be fully human (1 Cor. 15:21; 1 Tim. 2:5). The Gospels provide narrative presentations of these realities. As one born of Mary, Jesus is fully human. Yet the natural relation between Adam and all humanity is interrupted in the case of Jesus, since Jesus is born of a *virgin*. Adam did not represent Jesus. This supernatural birth ensures both the full humanity of Jesus and his freedom from the original sin and guilt that affects all natural descendants of Adam. Luke explicitly links the virgin birth to the holiness of Jesus.[2] Gabriel tells Mary, "The Holy Spirit will come upon you, and the power of the Most High will overshadow you; therefore the child to be born will be called holy—the Son of God" (Luke 1:35).

The virgin birth has significant implications for salvation. It helps explain the sinlessness of Jesus and highlights Jesus's role as the head of a new humanity. Just as the Spirit hovered

---

2. See also Amandus Polanus von Polansdorf, *Syntagma Theologiae Christianae* (Hanover: Wechel, 1615), §6.14 (p. 366).

over the world at creation, so the Spirit overshadows Mary and brings about a new creation in her womb.[3] And to speak of the new creation of humanity reminds us of the garden of Eden and the goal set before Adam of eternal life on the condition of perfect obedience. That possibility seems to have been lost with the fall of Adam. Because of sin, no one who had ever been born since Adam could meet the requirement of perfect obedience: not Noah (a preacher of righteousness who stood at the beginning of a new creation after the flood), not Moses (who was not even allowed to enter the promised land), and not David (a man after God's own heart, though his failures are well known). Not even Enoch or Elijah, neither of whom ever died, could meet the standard necessary for eternal life. To be sure, the experience of eternal life was a reality for true believers before the coming of Christ, but this was not because anyone had personally met the requisite standard for eternal life. Instead, eternal life is granted by the grace of God (even to believers in the Old Testament), but it is always dependent on *someone* meeting the requirement of perfect obedience.

But Jesus, conceived by the power and holiness of the Spirit, is protected from the sin of Adam and is in a position, as the head of new humanity, to realize the entire obedience never before (or since) realized in world history. His birth marks a new creation. The baptism and temptation episodes that follow are important for understanding Jesus's perfect obedience, so we look at them both now in more detail.

Baptism of Jesus

The baptism of Jesus is also important for understanding his obedience and the way it benefits others. John the Baptist came

3. Sinclair B. Ferguson, *The Holy Spirit*, CCT (Downers Grove, IL: InterVarsity, 1996), 38–39.

preaching repentance and administered a baptism of repentance for the forgiveness of sins (Mark 1:4; Luke 3:3). It is clear in the Gospels that Jesus had no need to repent for his own sins. John himself tried to forbid Jesus from being baptized (Matt. 3:14). Jesus comes to John's baptism as one who is—remarkably— free from sin.

If Jesus had no need for forgiveness, then why was he baptized? Jesus submitted to John's baptism as a representative who identified with God's people in their need for forgiveness. Jesus's baptism shows his solidarity with his people, as he enters into the waters representing forgiveness on behalf of those whose sins he would bear himself. In the Gospel of John, John the Baptist identifies Jesus as the Lamb of God who takes away the sin of the world (John 1:29).

The baptism John administered could not actually take away sin, but it anticipated God's definitive washing of his people from sin. This ultimate washing is only accomplished through the work of Jesus Christ. The representative (or *vicarious*) nature of Jesus's baptism shows us the representative nature of Jesus's entire obedience. In fact, the baptism itself is an aspect of that obedience, as Jesus responds appropriately to the prophetic call given to Israel at that time.

Put simply, Jesus is the substance to which John's baptism points. Jesus did not need forgiveness because he was sinless. But he did come to take away sin (Matt. 1:21; John 1:29). He could not take away sin if he had sins of his own that had to be atoned for (see Heb. 7:27). Only on the basis of Jesus's perfect obedience could forgiveness of sins be granted. John preached about this; Jesus achieved it. Jesus's baptism helps us see that just as his baptism was for the benefit of others, so too his obedience was for the benefit of others.

Jesus's baptism also demonstrates his representative role as Messiah. The baptism is the occasion for the Father's pronouncement of his pleasure in the beloved Son, further confirming that the baptism was an aspect of Jesus's obedience. When Jesus is baptized, the Holy Spirit descends. The Spirit was already with Christ from his conception through his childhood.[4] And yet here, as Jesus embarks upon a new stage in his public ministry, he is anointed in a new way with the Spirit, equipping him for his public work and his spiritual battle with the devil.

By obeying the call to participate in John the Baptist's divinely authorized baptism, Jesus identifies with God's people in their estate of sin and need for forgiveness, though he himself has no need for forgiveness. This act of solidarity is fitting for a representative who has come to save his people from their sins. Jesus is also anointed and empowered by the Holy Spirit for his messianic task, including the task of persevering in obedience. As the obedience of a representative and Adamic figure, Jesus's obedience can be counted representatively for others.

The Fully Obedient Son of God

Jesus Obeys in the Face of Temptation

We look now at some specific passages that highlight the representative obedience of Jesus. One of the most obvious is the temptation narrative, where Jesus obeys when tempted by the devil. Perhaps it is familiar to read this encounter as an example for us when we are tempted, especially in Matthew and Luke, where Jesus responds three times to the devil from specific texts of Scripture. Jesus's responses do indeed show us an effective way to face temptation: we should respond from Scripture.

But Jesus's temptations are more than only an example for his followers. Jesus's obedience in the face of temptation is primarily a key juncture in world history when God's Messiah fends off a frontal assault from the devil. In this pivotal spiritual

4. See Bavinck, *RD*, 3:292–93.

battle at the outset of his ministry, Jesus is the holy champion who overcomes sin by means of his obedience.

Luke's genealogy helps us understand that Jesus's obedience in the face of temptation is the obedience of a new Adam. This is evident in the way that Luke's temptation account follows immediately after the genealogy that traces Jesus as Son of God all the way back to Adam as son of God (Luke 3:38). By serving as a narrative bridge connecting the baptism of God's Son with the obedience of God's Son, Luke's genealogy highlights Jesus's obedience as the new Adam.

The role of the Spirit in Jesus's life can help us appreciate this representative obedience as well. The Spirit who anoints Jesus at his baptism soon leads him into the wilderness so that Jesus may be tempted by the devil (Matt. 4:1; Mark 1:12; Luke 4:1). Yet the Spirit also empowers Jesus for his obedience in the face of temptation. This is especially clear in Luke, as Jesus enters temptation full of the Spirit (4:1) and returns in the power of the Spirit after being tempted (4:14). The same Spirit who anoints Jesus with power for his ministry enables this representative to obey on behalf of his people. Throughout his ministry Jesus will be empowered by the Holy Spirit for good works (Acts 10:38), including the casting out of demons (Matt. 12:28).

The obedience Jesus embodies in the face of the devil's temptations is the obedience that we as sinful humans could not offer. This is attested in the way that Jesus's obedience reminds the readers of Israel's disobedience in their wilderness wanderings. Israel failed as God's son in the wilderness. In contrast, Jesus successfully obeys in the wilderness as God's Son. In two of the three temptations, the devil explicitly tests the *sonship* of Jesus. When the devil asks Jesus to turn stones into bread, Jesus responds from Deuteronomy 8:3, a passage that calls Israel to obey *as the son of God* even in the midst of difficulty (see 8:5–6). Israel failed in this task; Jesus obeyed. This sonship focus and the temptation to *eat* in the *wilderness* also recall

Adam's first sin—*eating* the forbidden fruit in the *garden*—and the desolation that resulted from his sin. Adam failed in his task; Jesus obeyed. The temptation of Jesus revealed what was in his heart (see Deut. 8:2, 16). He passed with flying colors. The obedience of Jesus in the wilderness temptation is the obedience of the Son of God who overcomes the disobedience of Israel and Adam.

The unparalleled obedience of Jesus is not only important for biblical history; it is cosmically significant.[5] The temptation episode represents a decisive turning point in world history: now the Son of God obeys God fully, refusing the allures of sin and clinging to the Word of God. Jesus's obedience in the face of temptation also shows us the unity of his active and passive obedience. For in the temptation Jesus actively resists the devil and submits to his Father, even as he suffers the lack of sustenance in the wilderness (see Mark 1:12–13).

The uniqueness of Jesus's perfect obedience in the face of temptation underscores Jesus's perfect obedience as God's covenantal Son. Jesus's obedience not only *surpasses* that of Israel and Adam, but *overcomes* their disobedience. This obedience was necessary to save a sinful people. To put it starkly, "If Jesus had here [i.e., in the temptation] (or indeed at any other time) lost in the conflict, God's whole plan of redemption in Him would have been defeated."[6]

Jesus Obeys and Binds the Strong Man

Jesus's obedience in his temptation sets the stage for his ministry that follows. From this point, it is clear that Jesus is the *fully obedient* Son of God, and his Spirit-enabled power goes hand in hand with his Spirit-enabled, entire obedience.

5. See Ferguson, *Holy Spirit*, 48; Geerhardus Vos, *Biblical Theology: Old and New Testaments* (1948; repr., Edinburgh: Banner of Truth, 1975), 320–21.
6. Norval Geldenhuys, *Commentary on the Gospel of Luke*, NICNT (Grand Rapids: Eerdmans, 1951), 158.

No spiritual opposition is able to stand against Jesus, for Jesus is the holy Son of God.

This brings us back to John the Baptist's testimony that a "stronger one" would come after him, who would baptize with the Holy Spirit and fire (Matt. 3:11; Mark 1:7–8; Luke 3:16). Jesus later speaks of himself as the stronger man, albeit cryptically. In one of the key parables that explains Jesus's ministry, he speaks of his role as the "stronger one" who binds the strong man (the devil). The strong man keeps people in captivity, and only the stronger one can bind the strong man and release the people kept in captivity. When the stronger one comes, he plunders the house, or kingdom, of the strong man.

How does Jesus bind the strong man? He does so in large measure by his obedience. This is especially clear in Mark, where the parable of the binding of the strong man (Mark 3:22–30) forms a literary frame with the obedience of Jesus in his temptation (1:12–13). In both stories, the main characters are Jesus, the devil, and the Holy Spirit,[7] and the earlier story explains the later story, along with much of the material in between. In Mark 3 Jesus responds to the charge that his authority comes from the devil himself (3:22, 30). Jesus instead shows that the conflict of kingdoms apparent in his ministry reveals that he is attacking the devil and is not in league with the devil. This is clear already from Jesus's opposition to the devil at the outset of his public ministry. Jesus's obedience in the face of temptation is apparently the initial binding of the strong man.[8] Jesus binds the devil by obeying his Father.

The binding of the strong man highlights the benefits of Jesus's obedience *for us*. In the ensuing verses Jesus goes on to

---

7. See Elizabeth E. Shively, *Apocalyptic Imagination in the Gospel of Mark: The Literary and Theological Role of Mark 3:22–30*, BZNW 189 (Berlin: de Gruyter, 2012), 43.

8. Ernest Best, *The Temptation and the Passion: The Markan Soteriology*, 2nd ed., SNTSMS 2 (Cambridge: Cambridge University Press, 1990), 12.

say that *because* he binds the strong man, *therefore* every sin and blasphemy will be forgiven (Mark 3:28–29).[9] This logic is implicit in Mark, but is even stronger in Matthew, where Jesus says "because of this" (*dia touto*, Matt. 12:31)—that is, because Jesus has bound the strong man (12:29)—all sins and blasphemies can be forgiven. There is no one whose authority transcends that of the Son of God, and forgiveness is offered on the basis of his perfect work.

The binding of the strong man shows us that Jesus came to destroy the works of the devil (1 John 3:8), securing forgiveness of sins. He does this by means of his obedience.

The Lord's Prayer and Our Lord's Obedience

The unique, representative obedience of Jesus may also be alluded to in the Lord's Prayer. This is evident, for example, in the petition that we might not be led into temptation (Matt. 6:13; see also Luke 11:4). When we pray, "Lead us not into temptation," we are asking to be protected from situations in which the devil would tempt us. This is consistent with the danger in view in Matthew 26:41 ("Watch and pray that you may not enter into temptation"), where the disciples are found sleeping instead of praying.[10] It is Satan who tempts us, for God does not tempt anyone (James 1:13). This petition therefore is primarily a prayer that we might not be overcome by sin.

The main point I wish to focus on, however, is the contrast between what the disciples are to pray and Jesus's own experience. Whereas the disciples are to pray that God would not lead them into temptation, Jesus, as the anointed representative of his people, is led by the Spirit into the wilderness for the express purpose of being tempted by the devil (Matt. 4:1). We therefore must read the petition in Matthew 6 in light of

9. The exception is blasphemy against the Holy Spirit, which is, in brief, to reject Jesus and his work (Mark 3:22, 30).
10. See Tertullian, *Prayer* 7.

the temptations of Jesus that precede it in Matthew 4. What was proper for Jesus, as the champion of our faith—facing the devil's temptations in the wilderness—is not proper for those who follow him by faith. Instead, the disciples are to take refuge by faith in the one who has already proved decisively obedient in the face of temptation.

This approach also makes sense of the second half of the petition: "Deliver us from evil" (Matt. 6:13), which is probably best translated as *deliver us from the evil one* (i.e., the devil). When Jesus was led into the wilderness to be tempted, he obeyed and bound the strong man. In contrast, the disciples of Jesus are not called personally to overcome the strong man. Instead, the disciples pray to be delivered from the evil one by placing their faith in the one who has already overcome the devil. John Calvin captured the sentiment well: "It is not in our power to engage that great warrior the devil in combat, or to bear his force and onslaught."[11]

At the end of the Lord's Prayer we are therefore reminded clearly of the Savior who keeps us from evil[12] and who is presupposed in the entire prayer.

Lifelong, Necessary Obedience

In addition to Jesus's obedience in his baptism and temptation, the Gospels speak of Jesus's obedience more expansively. Jesus is obedient in various ways throughout his life, and these ways provide additional windows into Jesus's representative obedience. Again, it's more than just the death of Christ which is necessary for salvation; the implication is that Jesus's *entire* obedience is also necessary for others' salvation. Here we'll

11. John Calvin, *Institutes of the Christian Religion*, ed. John T. McNeill, trans. Ford Lewis Battles, 2 vols., LCC 20–21 (Philadelphia: Westminster, 1960), 3.20.46 (2:914).
12. See John 17:12–15 with 1 John 5:18; see also 2 Thess. 3:2–3.

consider the theology of fulfillment in Matthew and the "it is necessary" (*dei*) statements in the Gospels, especially in Luke.

Fulfillment in Matthew

Matthew first speaks of fulfillment in relation to Jesus's baptism when Jesus answers John's hesitation to baptize him by stating that his baptism is fitting to fulfill all righteousness (Matt. 3:15). We have seen that Jesus submits to baptism as a representative, one who has no need personally for forgiveness. The righteousness Jesus speaks of here is something he accomplishes on behalf of others. This is consistent with the use of "righteousness" (*dikaiosyne*) throughout Matthew, which refers to what God requires of humanity (Matt. 5:6, 10, 20; 6:1, 33; 21:32). "To fulfill *all* righteousness" most likely refers to Jesus's accomplishment of *every aspect* of what God requires of humanity.

Further supporting this approach is the way Matthew uses the term "fulfill" (*pleroo*), which is a favorite term of his Gospel to speak about the way that Christ has accomplished salvation.[13] In addition to fulfilling all righteousness, Jesus is more often described as fulfilling Scripture by means of his obedience. This is apparent in Matthew's ten famous Old Testament fulfillment citations (Matt. 1:22–23; 2:15, 17–18, 23; 4:14–16; 8:17; 12:17–21; 13:35; 21:4–5; 27:9–10). These fulfillment citations highlight that the obedience of Jesus is antithetical to, and is likewise the answer to, the perennial disobedience of God's people. They indicate that every aspect of Jesus's life conforms to Scripture. Jesus offers the obedience that no one else was able to offer, and this is the means by which he accomplishes salvation.

One of the fulfillment citations that show how Jesus's obedience overcomes the sinfulness of previous generations is the

---

13. For what follows see Brandon D. Crowe, "Fulfillment in Matthew as Eschatological Reversal," *WTJ* 75 (2013): 111–27.

citation of Psalm 78:2 in Matthew 13:35. This verse is about Jesus's practice of speaking in parables: "This was to fulfill what was spoken by the prophet: 'I will open my mouth in parables; I will utter what has been hidden since the foundation of the world.'" The broader context of Psalm 78, which Matthew assumes and invokes when he cites a portion of the psalm, is important for understanding its relationship to the obedience of Christ. Psalm 78 extensively recounts the disobedience of Israel throughout its history. Psalm 78:6–8 warns that future generations must not be like previous generations who were stubborn and rebellious. The remainder of the psalm's seventy-two verses speak of failure after failure of the Israelites to be faithful to their covenant Lord, despite the wonders he did on Israel's behalf.

The instruction described in this psalm (78:2) is fulfilled in Jesus's teaching by means of parables in Matthew 13:35. Matthew emphasizes the greatness of the mystery of the kingdom— that which was formerly hidden—now revealed (see 13:16–17, 52). *What was formerly hidden* refers not to completely new meanings of Old Testament passages that were previously inaccessible. On the contrary, Matthew indicates that the Old Testament teachings about Christ were there all along, and he draws attention to the details of how the various messianic hopes in the Old Testament all converge and coalesce in the person and work of Christor.[14] Therefore, Matthew 13 seems to allude to the obedience of Christ in contrast to and overcoming the disobedience of Israel in Psalm 78. Jesus speaks in parables not only to teach and produce both positive and negative results (Matt. 13:11–17; see also Isa. 6:9–10) but also to draw attention to his own obedience.

Matthew's fulfillment citations help us see that as the representative of his people, Jesus overcomes the sinfulness of his

---

14. See D. A. Carson, "Matthew," in *Matthew, Mark, Luke*, vol. 8 of *The Expositor's Bible Commentary*, ed. F. A. Gaebelein (Grand Rapids: Zondervan, 1984), 321–23.

people, and by so doing brings about the blessings that the prophets anticipated would come in the latter days.[15] These salvific blessings come on the coattails of Jesus's perfect obedience. As the one who must save his people from their sins (Matt. 1:21) and fulfill all righteousness (3:15), Jesus fulfills the Scriptures and overcomes the sinfulness of his people's history. He brings the new era of redemptive history in which the Messiah reigns, having overcome sin and death by his wide-ranging obedience. Matthew's fulfillment quotations show us both the need for Jesus to save his people from their sins and the glorious reality that he has done it—*fully*.

"It Is Necessary" (*Dei*)

The wide-ranging obedience of Jesus is also highlighted by many "it is necessary" (*dei*) statements in the Gospels. Luke is especially well known for his use of the term *dei*, which highlights what must be done for the accomplishment of salvation. These statements indicate a range of things that were necessary for Jesus to do to accomplish salvation. It was necessary for Jesus not only to die and rise again (see Luke 9:22; 13:33; 17:25; 22:37; 24:7, 26, 44–47) but also to be about the business of his father (2:49) as a twelve-year-old. It was necessary for Jesus to free a woman in bondage to Satan (13:16) and to complete his work "today and tomorrow" before finishing his course "on the third day" (13:32–33). It was necessary for Jesus to pursue Zacchaeus (19:5) because the Son of Man came to seek and to save the lost (19:10). Luke knows of no sharp division between the obedience of Jesus on the cross and the obedience of Jesus more broadly throughout his life and ministry. Jesus's entire obedience is necessary for salvation.

15. See, e.g., the end of exile and restoration (Isa. 40:1–11; 43:1–21; Ezek. 37:1–14), the new covenant (Jer. 31:31–34), the people reunited under one king (Ezek. 37:15–28), and the kingdom that would not end (Isa. 9:6–7; Dan. 2:44; Obad. 21).

The Gospel of John also highlights the necessity of Jesus's obedience. It is necessary (*dei*) for Jesus to be lifted up on the cross and in his resurrection (John 3:14; 12:34; 20:9). But it was also necessary for Jesus (and his disciples) to do the works of God while the time is right (9:4). Jesus himself spoke of his necessity to go through Samaria (4:4), which probably refers not simply to the best travel route, but to the work he had to do in Samaria, including the message he brought (see 4:24). As in Luke, so in John—Jesus's obedience beyond the cross was necessary for salvation.

This brief foray into the Gospel of John highlights the need to consider John's singular contributions in more detail.

Faith in the Obedient Son in the Gospel of John

The Gospel of John not only addresses the necessity of Jesus's work, but speaks of the way that we benefit from the obedience of Jesus—by faith.

Structural Cues in John: Seven Signs Focused on Life in Christ

John's Gospel highlights seven miraculous "signs" (*sēmeia*) of Jesus.[16] These seven signs are likely presented in a structured, parallel way (in a *chiasm*, which is arranged like the Greek character *chi* [X]). The first and last portions are parallel, then the second and next-to-last sections are parallel, and so forth, and the center of the chiasm is often the focal point. The chiastic structure of signs focuses attention on Jesus and his unique work as the fully obedient Son and points us to the life that is

16. My discussion of this structure is taken from Brandon D. Crowe, "The Chiastic Structure of Seven Signs in the Gospel of John: Revisiting a Neglected Proposal," *BBR* 28 (2018): 65–81, which builds on Marc Girard, "La composition structurelle des sept 'signes' dans le quatrième évangile," *Studies in Religion/Sciences Religieuses* 9 (1980): 315–24.

found in Christ by faith. A further benefit of identifying these as John's signs is that all seven of these events are explicitly identified as signs in the Gospel.

Chiastic Structure of Seven Signs in John

A Water, wine, cleansing, and blessed life (2:1–11; identified as a "sign" in 2:11)

  B Healing of a deathly ill child (4:43–54; identified as a "sign" in 4:54)

    C Healing of a lame man (5:1–16; included among the "signs" in 6:2)

      D Multiplication of bread (6:1–15; identified as a "sign" in 6:14, 26)

    C′ Healing of a blind man (9:1–6; included among the "signs" in 9:16)

  B′ Resuscitation of a dead man (11:1–44; identified as a "sign" in 12:18; see also 11:47)

A′ Water, blood, cleansing, and resurrection life (19:1–20:31; identified as a "sign" in 2:18–19; 20:30–31; see also 12:33; 18:32)

If John presents seven signs as a chiasm, the focal or pivot point is the feeding of the five thousand (6:1–15). This miracle encapsulates to a significant degree the entire Gospel of John, which is focused on signs that lead to life in Christ (20:30–31). The significance of the feeding of the multitudes comes in an extended speech of Jesus—the Bread of Life Discourse (6:26–59). The physical bread Jesus provided points to the spiritual bread—Jesus himself—who has come down from heaven and on whom we must feed by faith (e.g., 6:29, 35–40, 48–51, 57–58).

Life in Union with the Obedient Son

In the Bread of Life Discourse Jesus exhorts his audience not to work for food that will pass away, but for the food that comes down from heaven (John 6:27, 33). He also tells his audience what the work is that God requires: to believe in the one whom God has sent (6:29). This is ironic: the work that God requires is no work at all; it is instead to look away from ourselves and trust in the one whom God has sent. To believe in the one who was sent means trusting in the one who came to do the will of his Father (6:38), whose food is to do the will of God (4:34), and who always does what pleases his Father (8:29; see also 5:30). Faith means looking away from ourselves to the one who saves us by his work. We are to feed by faith on the true bread from heaven, the Son of Man, who gives us his flesh and blood to eat and drink (6:51–56). We are to abide by faith in the Son of Man that we might have life. This language of eating and drinking, along with the verb "abide" (*menō*), speaks of our union with Christ.[17]

When Jesus speaks in John 6 of believing in the heavenly bread, this means we must believe in the perfectly obedient Son of God. This is the means by which we can experience eternal, resurrection life (see esp. 5:24–25; 6:40, 54). This resurrection life also points to the perfect obedience of Jesus, for Jesus's own resurrection was predicated on his perfect obedience, as we will explore further in the next two chapters. Jesus, the one who perfectly did the will of his Father, is the resurrection and the life (11:25). It will also be important to discuss exactly what *faith* and *believe* mean. These terms have received quite a bit of attention in recent years. I'll return to this discussion of *faith* in chapter 8.

In sum, John's Gospel highlights the necessity of Jesus's obedience for salvation by showing the need to believe and abide in the Son of God for eternal life. Eternal life comes from the work of our Savior. Indeed, in John eternal life is characterized

---

17. See Grant Macaskill, *Union with Christ in the New Testament* (Oxford: Oxford University Press, 2014), 216.

as *resurrection* life, which points us to the one who laid down his life that he might take it up again (10:17–18). His works are evidence that the Father dwells in Jesus and works through him (14:10–11). Faith in this fully obedient Son yields eternal life (20:30–31). Readers must perceive by faith that to which the signs point. And ultimately the *that* to which the signs point is *he to whom* the signs point: the Son who has come down from heaven and has the authority to grant eternal life, which comes through the laying down and taking up of his own life.[18]

By focusing on the life that comes through faith in the glorious Son of God—the one who obeyed his Father in all things—we again see in narrative fashion the importance of Jesus's perfect obedience for eternal life.

Unity of Obedience and Sacrifice

The Gospels also focus, to a significant degree, on the death of Christ. My argument that Jesus is portrayed in the Gospels as accomplishing salvation by being perfectly obedient is not intended to undermine the importance of Jesus's death. It is, rather, to underscore the unity of Jesus's life and death. I argued earlier (in ch. 2) that we cannot divide the perfect obedience of Jesus into parts that belong to his life and parts that belong to his death. Jesus's entire life (including his death on the cross) is active obedience, and his entire life (including his death on the cross) is passive obedience. Certainly it's necessary for Jesus to be a spotless lamb of God to serve as a sacrifice. But the Gospels speak about Jesus's obedience as being more than only a necessary prerequisite for a fitting sacrifice.

This brings us back to Matthew, who shows how in Jesus love and obedience—or mercy and sacrifice—are coterminous. There is no disparity between them. A key text for Matthew

18. These final two sentences are adapted from Crowe, "Chiastic Structure," 81.

is Hosea 6:6: "I desire mercy, and not sacrifice." This is the only Old Testament text quoted more than once by Matthew (9:13; 12:7). These quotations come in Jesus's first two conflicts with the Pharisees—they honored God with their lips, but their hearts were far from him (Matt. 15:8; see also Isa. 29:13). In other words, their sacrifices may have been right according to the letter, but there was a disconnect between their outward obedience and their inner spiritual condition. They were like whitewashed tombs filled with dead people's bones (Matt. 23:27). Despite their rigorous tithing, the Pharisees neglected the weightier matters of the law—justice, mercy, and faith(fulness) (23:23).

In contrast to the Pharisees—whose obedience was insufficient—Jesus fulfilled the two great commandments of loving God and loving one's neighbor (Matt. 22:37–39). Hosea 6:6 is about the need to love God and neighbor, not simply the offering of (hollow) sacrifices. In light of what God requires, it is striking that Jesus embodied the mercy (or *love*) that God requires. In Jesus there is no dichotomy between internal disposition and external obedience, no division between mercy and sacrifice, since the one who sacrificed his own life for the inauguration of the new covenant (see 26:28) is also the one who loved God most fully. Both aspects are integrated in the obedient life of Jesus. He alone is suited to give his life as a ransom (Matt. 20:28; Mark 10:45).

The dichotomy of the Pharisees provides a stark contrast to the integrated obedience of Jesus, but it also illustrates the broader point we have seen in many ways: Jesus's obedience is qualitatively different. Even those who walked in God's ways in the Gospels—think of Zechariah, Elizabeth, Mary, Joseph, Simeon, and Anna in Luke 1–2—were not perfect. They too looked outside of themselves for salvation. To make this observation is to state the obvious, yet sometimes we need to consider the obvious from a different angle. What is required for salvation? Salvation requires not only forgiveness of sins (see Luke 1:77) but also the right to eternal life. This means that Zechariah, Elizabeth, Mary, Joseph, Simeon, and Anna—along with all true believers—need an obedient representative to be fully righteous before God. They need a new Adam (3:38).

Conclusion

The Gospels show us how Jesus came to save his people from their sins (Matt. 1:21). He does this not only by dying for sins but also by living a life of perfect obedience. Jesus obeyed as a representative, which means his obedience can be counted vicariously on behalf of others. His perfect obedience does more than only qualify him to serve as a perfect sacrifice; it also realizes what Adam failed to do.

The Gospels do many things. They teach us about how to live as disciples. They show how Jesus fulfills the Old Testament. They speak about the kingdom of God. They narrate the death of Christ. But throughout the Gospels Jesus perfectly obeys his Father. Perhaps this is so obvious that we may miss its implications. But when we read these four narratives of Jesus in concert with the explanations of his work elsewhere in Scripture, it becomes that much clearer that Jesus's unique obedience was necessary for salvation.

We have seen this already in Paul's Letters; now we have seen it in the Gospels. In the next chapter we will see how the Letter to the Hebrews adds further insight into Jesus's obedience in relationship to his perfect sacrifice.

6

THE OBEDIENCE OF
THE PERFECT PRIEST

Fundraising can be a long and arduous process. Maybe it's easier at the beginning, but getting over the last hump may seem to take forever. The final stretch seems to extend indefinitely beyond the horizon, which makes it all the sweeter when you finally do reach the goal. The last donation, the one to put you over the top, is the most rewarding, and—it seems—the most important.

True though the feeling is, the final donation is not really more important than the first. If you don't work hard to raise the funds before the end, there will be no satisfying, climactic moment to celebrate at the end. Earlier contributions toward meeting the goal are just as important as later contributions. Both are necessary.

This holistic perspective helps us understand the relationship between Jesus's lifelong obedience and his obedient death on the cross. This is an issue that the Epistle to the Hebrews, in particular, helps us understand. Hebrews has much to say about the final sacrifice of Christ, but Hebrews also helps us understand the obedience of Christ more broadly in relation to salvation. In fact, Hebrews contains some of the most explicit and moving passages about the obedience of Christ anywhere in Scripture.[1] The obedience of Jesus is certainly seen with particular clarity on the cross, but Hebrews is further testimony to the integrated obedience of Jesus. The perfect obedience of Jesus in his incarnate work includes all that he did to save his people from their sins, being made perfect even through suffering. Key passages I will address in this chapter include Hebrews 2, 5, and 10.

Hebrews also joins other New Testament voices in highlighting the significance of Christ's resurrection for salvation and as that which vindicates his perfect obedience. Christ serves now as the heavenly, exalted high priest, and this is a constant attestation of the perfection of his life of obedience. I tease out these issues in what follows.

Need for a Priest

One of the key categories that Hebrews uses to highlight the obedience of Jesus is his role as the great high priest.[2] Hebrews discusses Christ as priest extensively, and only in Hebrews is the term *priest* used expressly for Jesus.[3] The overall concern

1. See John Murray, *Redemption Accomplished and Applied* (Grand Rapids: Eerdmans, 1955), 22–24, noted by Peter J. Gentry and Stephen G. Wellum, *Kingdom through Covenant: A Biblical-Theological Understanding of the Covenants*, 2nd ed. (Wheaton: Crossway, 2018), 776–77.

2. What follows (including the section on the Gospels) is adapted from Brandon D. Crowe, "Jesus, Our Great High Priest," *Credo Magazine* 6, no. 2 (2016): 16–21.

3. Some believe Hebrews teaches that Christ is a priest *exclusively* in heaven. Though the author of Hebrews uses the terminology of *priest* for Jesus's heavenly activity, the *concepts* of priesthood are present in his work on earth as well.

of Hebrews may even be to explain the significance of Jesus's high priesthood, especially in light of Hebrews 8:1: "Now the [main] point in what we are saying is this: we have such a high priest, one who is seated at the right hand of the throne of the Majesty in heaven."[4]

We all require a priest to approach God, though this is not the same thing as saying we need an earthly, (merely) human priest. Hebrews emphasizes that Jesus Christ himself is our great high priest, who serves in heaven, and he has no rivals. But this high priest is the same one who was made low for us and for our salvation, obeying and suffering for sin. The author of Hebrews takes great care to explain the obedience and suffering of Christ, because these degrading experiences might otherwise seem to be unfitting for one who is so glorious. But the grind of Jesus's obedience, even in the face of suffering, was necessary for our acceptance before God and is also necessary for the acceptance of Jesus's final sacrifice. Understanding the way that the author teases out the relationship between Jesus's life and death will help us appreciate the need for Jesus's perfect obedience to take away sin.

Incarnation and Perfect Obedience

The Divine Son of God (Hebrews 1)

In the incarnation the eternal, unchangeable Son of God took a human nature in a personal and permanent union. In this sense, the incarnation assumes the divinity and preexistence of the Son of God, who was not created when he was born of Mary. He has always existed. This is the way that Hebrews opens, and the author of Hebrews closely relates Jesus's divinity

---

4. Modified from the ESV. See further Richard B. Gaffin Jr., "The Priesthood of Christ: A Servant in the Sanctuary," in *The Perfect Saviour: Key Themes in Hebrews*, ed. Jonathan Griffiths (Nottingham: Inter-Varsity, 2012), 56–57.

to his role as prophet, priest, and king. Hebrews 1:1–4 can be arranged as follows:[5]

> A Long ago, at many times and in many ways, God spoke to our fathers by the prophets, but in these last days he has spoken to us by his Son (1:1–2a),
> > B whom he appointed the heir of all things (1:2b),
> > > C through whom also he created the world (1:2c).
> > > > D He is the radiance of the glory of God (1:3a)
> > > > D′ and the exact imprint of his nature (1:3b),
> > > C′ and he upholds the universe by the word of his power (1:3c).
> > B′ After making purification for sins, he sat down at the right hand of the Majesty on high (1:3d),
> A′ having become as much superior to angels as the name he has inherited is more excellent than theirs (1:4).

The structure could be summarized:

> A Son's superiority to the prophets (1:1–2a)
> > B Son as royal heir (1:2b)
> > > C Son's work of creation (1:2c)
> > > > D Son as the radiance of God's glory (1:3a)
> > > > D′ Son as the exact imprint of God's nature (1:3b)
> > > C′ Son's work of providence (1:3c)
> > B′ Son as royal priest (1:3d)
> A′ Son's superiority to the angels (1:4)

---

5. This structure represents my own assessment; a virtually identical structure is found in Lane G. Tipton, "Christology in Colossians 1:15–20 and Hebrews 1:1–4: An Exercise in Biblico-Systematic Theology," in *Resurrection and Eschatology: Theology in Service of the Church; Essays in Honor of Richard B. Gaffin Jr.*, ed. Lane G. Tipton and Jeffrey C. Waddington (Phillipsburg, NJ: P&R, 2008), 179–81.

The central focus of this structure (D/D′) highlights the divinity of the Son. This provides the framework for understanding the work of the Son in Hebrews, including his obedience as a man. Some also see already in Hebrews 1:1–4 the theology of Christ as new Adam. He is not only the divine Son, but the Son whose obedience as a man qualifies him to rule over creation, as Adam had been tasked in the beginning.[6] Hebrews 1:1–4 also sets the stage for an apparent contradiction later when the author discusses the suffering and death of the glorious Son of God. How could the eternal Son of God suffer and die? The author will insist this was in fact most fitting, for through the incarnate obedience of the divine Son of God death itself is defeated (2:10–15), leading to the realization of God's glorious vision for humanity.

These opening verses proceed to highlight the priesthood of the Son (Heb. 1:3d), which is primarily understood as a heavenly, high priesthood in light of his resurrection (though also assuming Christ's sacrificial death). Jesus has made purification for sins and taken his seat at God's right hand (1:3d; see also 1:2b; Ps. 110:1). This assumes his resurrection. The author will later explain how, as a royal priest-king like Melchizedek, Jesus always lives and intercedes for us in heaven (Heb. 4:14–16; 6:19–20; 7:22–8:6; 9:24). This heavenly high priesthood is therefore something new which was realized after Christ's death and resurrection; it is thus possible because of the perfection of the Son's obedience. Though his obedience involved suffering, it led to glory incomparable.

The Son's Obedience and Suffering (Hebrews 2, 5)

The author of Hebrews emphasizes the glory of the Son in Hebrews 1, contrasting his glory with that of the angels. He

6. G. K. Beale and Benjamin L. Gladd, *The Story Retold: A Biblical-Theological Introduction to the New Testament* (Downers Grove, IL: IVP Academic, 2020), 368–70.

then discusses how it's not angels who will rule in the world to come, but humanity (2:5–8). Yet here arises something that doesn't seem to mesh with our experience of reality: if God created the world to be subject to humanity (see Ps. 8), then why do we not see this realized around us? Why is there still difficulty and sin and chaos and rebellion in the world?

The answer is found in Jesus: though we don't presently see all things subject to humanity, we do see Jesus, who is crowned with the glory and honor envisioned in Psalm 8. After suffering and dying, he has risen and reigns as king over all creation, thereby realizing the calling and goal of humanity. And it's crucial to understand the *redemptive-historical reason why* Jesus has been crowned with glory and honor: he was crowned with glory and honor *because* of his obedience and, in Hebrews 2:9, because of his suffering unto death.

This obedience unto death is explained in more detail in Hebrews 2:10–18. It is fitting for the one who is supreme over all to be made perfect through suffering, in order that he might lead many sons to glory. Jesus is the forerunner, pioneer, or champion (= *archēgos*) of salvation.[7] However we choose to translate *archēgos*, the term is always used in the New Testament to refer to the resurrection of Jesus (Acts 3:15; 5:31; Heb. 2:10; 12:2)[8] and emphasizes the solidarity of Jesus with his people. Jesus's victory over suffering—especially by means of his resurrection and defeat of death—enables him to lead his people to eternal life. His resurrection assumes the obedience of his entire life, though Hebrews here emphasizes the solidarity of Jesus with the suffering of his people. Jesus overcame suffering in his body and is able to help those who suffer.

7. *Archēgos* is translated in various ways. For options see BDAG, "ἀρχηγός," 138–39. "Champion" is preferred by William L. Lane, *Hebrews 1–8*, WBC 47A (Nashville: Nelson, 1991), 56–57.
8. See also Paul Ellingworth, *The Epistle to the Hebrews: A Commentary on the Greek Text*, NIGTC (Grand Rapids: Eerdmans, 1993), 160.

Why is this *fitting*? It is fitting for a human to rule over God's creation, and therefore it was fitting for the Son as a human to obey and overcome death by his resurrection, thereby ruling forever. Jesus's resurrection required his obedience in the face of suffering, which was necessary to defeat the devil, who holds people in captivity to the fear of death (Heb. 2:14–15). The Son had "to make propitiation for the sins of the people" (2:17), and this required him to be made like his people in every way (apart from sin). Because he obeyed, even when he suffered, Jesus is qualified to serve as a merciful and faithful high priest (2:18). He has conquered the devil and removed the curse of sin.

When the author of Hebrews speaks of being made "perfect" (see 2:10), this refers not to any need to make the eternal Son of God "perfect" in his *essence*. Nor does it refer to the need to overcome some moral uncleanness of the Son in his incarnate state. As we have seen, Jesus was born in holiness. He was not born with a sinful nature, and he was not drawn internally toward sin. Instead, being made perfect in Hebrews refers to the way that Jesus's obedience and suffering enabled him to serve as a perfect, final high priest for his people in the era of new covenant fulfillment.[9]

The obedience of Jesus and its relation to his perfection as priest is further addressed in Hebrews 5:7–10, in a way that echoes 2:10–18.[10] The writer speaks summarily of the days of Jesus's flesh (5:7), which invokes Jesus's incarnate life as a whole.[11] Though "prayers and supplications" in 5:7 probably refers specifically to those before the cross in the garden of Gethsemane,[12] it could refer more broadly to the acceptable

9. See also Moisés Silva, "Perfection and Eschatology in Hebrews," *WTJ* 39 (1976): 60–71.

10. F. F. Bruce, *The Epistle to the Hebrews*, NICNT (Grand Rapids: Eerdmans, 1964), 97–98.

11. See Ellingworth, *Hebrews*, 287.

12. E.g., Bavinck, *RD*, 3:388.

prayers of Jesus in concert with his lifelong piety.[13] Either way, there can be little doubt that during his earthly sojourn, Jesus often devoted himself to prayer, as is clear in the Gospels. Not only at the end of his life, but throughout his life, Jesus was fully obedient, which is a major reason why Jesus is a better priest than all others. As a priest already in the days of his lowliness and suffering, Jesus offered up prayers and supplications, and these were accepted (5:7).[14] No sacrifice for himself was necessary (see 7:27).

Hebrews closely relates the suffering of Jesus in his earthly life to his bodily sacrifice. Jesus was made perfect through suffering, and this was consummated on the cross, which yielded his resurrection (5:9–10). Yet Jesus suffered throughout his life, by which he was trained in and grew in obedience (5:8). John Murray captured it well: "It is obedience learned through suffering, perfected through suffering, and consummated in the suffering of death upon the cross that defines his work and accomplishment as the author of salvation. It was by obedience he secured our salvation because it was by obedience he wrought the work that secured it."[15]

The author of Hebrews discusses the sacrificial death and heavenly ministry of Christ at great length. Though it may seem unfitting for the glorious Son of God to suffer and die, it is through suffering and death that Jesus could be perfected as the final, glorious high priest. By the obedience of his entire life, evident in his resurrection, Jesus offers the consummate sacrifice that seals his work, which further underscores the need for every aspect of his obedience. Only Jesus is a perfectly

13. See similarly Bruce, *Hebrews*, 100; David A. deSilva, *Perseverance in Gratitude: A Socio-Rhetorical Commentary on the Epistle "to the Hebrews"* (Grand Rapids: Eerdmans, 2000), 189–91 and 191n26; see also Lane, *Hebrews 1–8*, 119–20.

14. See Lane, *Hebrews 1–8*, 119. Jesus was heard—he was not *kept* from death but *saved* from death when he was raised from the dead. See further Lane, *Hebrews 1–8*, 120; deSilva, *Perseverance in Gratitude*, 190; Bavinck, *RD*, 3:387.

15. Murray, *Redemption Accomplished and Applied*, 24.

obedient priest who offers himself, overcoming death by his resurrection. This is explained further in Hebrews 10.

The Son's Delight to Do God's Will (Psalm 40 and Hebrews 10)

The relationship between Jesus's obedience and final sacrifice is also addressed in Hebrews 10, which discusses the nature of the new covenant sacrifice of Christ as Son and great high priest.[16] The sacrifice of Christ inaugurates the new and better covenant (Heb. 8–9), which has been perfected once and for all by the perfect priest, who did not need to offer a sacrifice first for himself (10:1–4, 10–14). This final sacrifice was possible because of Jesus's full-fledged obedience. This point is made from the quotation of Psalm 40:6–8 in Hebrews 10:5–7:

> Consequently, when Christ came into the world, he said, "Sacrifices and offerings you have not desired, but a body have you prepared for me; in burnt offerings and sin offerings you have taken no pleasure. Then I said, 'Behold, I have come to do your will, O God, as it is written of me in the scroll of the book.'"

These words of David echo the scriptural truth that God's delight is not primarily in external ritual acts, but in hearts that are truly committed to the Lord.[17] A frequent problem among God's people throughout Scripture is the disconnect between obedience and sacrifice. In other words, often the problem was not failure by God's people to offer sacrifices, but rather their hypocrisy—offering sacrifices while not conforming their lives to the law of God. Where true obedience is lacking, sacrifices don't please the Lord. Building on earlier discussions of Jesus's

16. Here I build on Brandon D. Crowe, "Reading Psalm 40 Messianically," *Reformed Faith and Practice* 2, no. 3 (December 2017): 31–44.
17. See 1 Sam. 15:22; Ps. 51:15–16; Prov. 21:3; Isa. 29:13; Hosea 6:6; Amos 5:21–24.

obedience in Hebrews, the citation of Psalm 40 in Hebrews 10 shows that the entire obedience of Christ in the incarnation overcomes the infelicitous dichotomy between sacrifice and obedience that was historically a problem for God's people. God desired his people to offer sacrifice in conjunction with love and obedience; he does not delight in mere ritual.

This dichotomy is problematic for Jeremiah (see Jer. 6:21–24; 7:1–34), who prophesies the need for a *new covenant* (31:31–34; see also Heb. 8:7), which is the focus of this section of Hebrews. In Jeremiah's new covenant, the dichotomy between internal and external religion would be overcome, because God's law would be written on his people's hearts (Jer. 31:31–34; see also 4:4; 9:25). This is preeminently true of Christ, on whose heart the law was written (see Ps. 40:8). The new covenant prophesied by Jeremiah is instituted on the basis of Jesus's full obedience.

As the fully obedient one, Christ offered himself as the final sacrifice. This was something that no other priest had ever been able to do, since all other priests had first to offer sacrifices for themselves (Heb. 7:27). Yet even the blood of goats and bulls was insufficient ultimately to take away sin (10:4). Therefore, Christ is the better, heavenly high priest (see 8:1–2); his final sacrifice is perfect and effectual (9:14, 28; 10:14). To be the perfect sacrifice without blemish, Jesus had to be fully devoted to God in every way. For God's law not only demands absence of sin but also demands the positive accomplishment of righteousness. To fulfill the law requires us to love God and neighbor (see Matt. 22:37–40), and even requires internal obedience (see Ps. 40:8 and Heb. 10:7).[18] Jesus obeyed perfectly in his body (i.e., as incarnate).

The emphasis on the *body* of Jesus in Hebrews 10 allows us to consider in more detail how the author of Hebrews relates

18. See Amandus Polanus von Polansdorf, *Syntagma Theologiae Christianae* (Hanover: Wechel, 1615), §6.10 (p. 350), §6.14 (p. 366).

Psalm 40 to Jesus as high priest. In his body, Jesus shared in our experience of suffering, qualifying him to serve as a merciful high priest (Heb. 4:14–16). His bodily sacrifice is in view in 10:10: "And by [God's] will we have been sanctified through the once-for-all offering of Jesus's body" (my translation). By offering himself as the final, effectual sacrifice, Jesus "eradicated the disparity between sacrifice and obedience."[19] His final sacrifice assumes the entire obedience he rendered in his body.

By his final, perfect sacrifice, Jesus brings the deliverance anticipated by David in Psalm 40. Just as Psalm 40 encourages us to look beyond God's deliverance of David in the past (40:1–3) to the full, final deliverance in the future (40:13–15), so the obedience of David in Psalm 40:6–8 also looks ahead to the fuller realization of the obedience of God's anointed king. David speaks about himself to some degree in Psalm 40 as the one who came to do what was written of him in the book (40:7). "Book" here from David's perspective probably refers largely to the laws for the king in Deuteronomy 17:14–20. David speaks as the Lord's anointed, the one who leads and protects the people of God against their enemies (see 17:20). For the people to prosper and the kingdom to persevere, the king must obey the Lord, trusting without pretension. David's actions are the actions of an anointed representative, who must know, meditate on, and walk by God's law (e.g., Pss. 1; 19). Yet the problems that persisted for David were due, at least in part, to his own iniquities (see Ps. 40:12).

It is not difficult to see, then, how the need for future deliverance in Psalm 40 is also coupled with the problem of imperfect obedience. The greater deliverance David anticipated comes by means of Jesus's greater obedience. Because he was a sinner, David needed sacrifices for himself (see 51:15–16). Jesus is greater than David because he does not need a sacrifice for

<hr />

19. See Lane, *Hebrews 1–8*, cxxxiv; Lane, *Hebrews 9–13*, WBC 47B (Nashville: Nelson, 2000), 266.

himself, nor did Jesus ever face a problem resulting from his own sinfulness. The author of Hebrews clearly reads Psalm 40 christologically (see 10:5—it is Christ who speaks Ps. 40:6–8 in reference to his incarnation), and the author has in view a more thoroughgoing obedience than was realized by David himself. Jesus's commitment to God's will, building on Psalm 40, points both to the perfect sacrifice of his death and also to his full conformity to the law of God (including Deut. 17). Only in Jesus are perfect obedience and perfect sacrifice united. And this results in final deliverance.[20]

Understanding Hebrews 10 as emphasizing Christ's full obedience to God's will in his life by no means undermines the sacrifice of his death. Instead, this approach understands a unity of obedience and sacrifice, which is consummated in his death and lends additional warrant for understanding the obedience of Christ to have both passive and active dimensions. For example, John Calvin observed that Jesus's sacrifice required his willing obedience: "No proper sacrifice to God could have been offered unless Christ, disregarding his own feelings, subjected and yielded himself wholly to his Father's will."[21] Redemption comes through the one who has come to do God's will fully,

20. Recently Benjamin J. Ribbens ("The Sacrifice God Desired: Psalm 40:6–8 in Hebrews 10," *NTS* 67 [2021]: 284–304) has engagingly argued that God's will in Heb. 10 is God's "soteriological will" (295), by which he means God's will for the final sacrifice in which he delights. Thus, Heb. 10:5–7 is primarily about Christ's sacrifice and secondarily about Christ's obedience. Yet it seems better not to separate sacrifice and obedience in this passage, since they are held so closely together in Christ. Psalm 40 reflects the broader biblical truth that God requires (and delights in) his people's true obedience, which is often contrasted with mere sacrifice or external rites. See further Brandon D. Crowe, *The Path of Faith: A Biblical Theology of Covenant and Law*, ESBT (Downers Grove, IL: IVP Academic, 2021), 71–74, 84–87, 108–9. Christ alone perfectly realizes this obedience, which has always been required (see, e.g., Heb. 2:5–18). Further, since Christ's obedience is *representative* obedience, it would also be appropriate to speak of his obedience as *soteriological*, for it is no less necessary for salvation than his final sacrifice and his ongoing, heavenly, high-priestly ministry.

21. John Calvin, *Institutes of the Christian Religion*, ed. John T. McNeill, trans. Ford Lewis Battles, 2 vols., LCC 20–21 (Philadelphia: Westminster, 1960), 2.16.5 (1:508).

Herman Bavinck on the Unity of Christ's Obedience

"Scripture regards the entire work of Christ as a fulfillment of God's law and a satisfaction of his demand. As prophet, priest, and king, in his birth and in his death, in his words and in his deeds, he always did God's will. He came into the world to do his will. The law of God is within his heart [Ps. 40:8]. His entire life was a life of complete obedience, a perfect sacrifice, a sweet odor to God."

—Herman Bavinck, *RD*, 3:394

---

which includes perfect conformity to the law and also serving, in his own body, as the final, effectual sacrifice.

Resurrection and Perfect Obedience in Hebrews

The perfect obedience of Jesus is also apparent in Hebrews in the way that Jesus serves as a *heavenly*—and therefore *resurrected*—high priest. Hebrews emphasizes that Jesus serves in the heavenly sanctuary, which means he must be living now, and his death was not his end. There is much to say about the nuances of this heavenly high priesthood, but I highlight it here because the heavenly high priesthood of Christ requires Jesus's resurrection, and the resurrection requires that sin had no claim on Jesus.

The heavenly resurrected priesthood of Jesus is apparent from the beginning of Hebrews, as we saw earlier with 1:1–4. Jesus made purification for sins and sat down at the right hand of the Majesty on high (1:3).[22] It is possible that 5:7 refers to

22. Further, when Hebrews speaks of Jesus coming into the world (*oikoumenē*, 1:6; see also 2:5), this probably refers to the heavenly world. See Lane, *Hebrews*

Jesus's resurrection in light of Jesus's godliness when the author says that Jesus prayed to the one who could save him "from death" (*ek thanatou*). Regardless of how we take 5:7, we have already seen that Hebrews 5 speaks of the full obedience of Jesus, as does Hebrews 2. More specifically, in 2:14 Jesus is victorious over the one who holds the power of death, which points to his victory over sin in tandem with his obedience. Similarly, the sacrifice of Jesus in Hebrews 10 opens up a living way behind the inner veil (6:19–20; 10:19–22). Jesus's perfect sacrifice yields life not only for him but for all those in him. He is a better priest than the Aaronic priesthood in the Old Testament, for his priesthood is based not on the law of lineage but on the power of an indestructible life (7:16). In other words, he lives forever.

In Hebrews 7:26, as well, the obedience of Jesus is tethered to his resurrection: "For it was indeed fitting that we should have such a high priest, holy, innocent, unstained, separated from sinners, and exalted above the heavens." This further shows us that the exaltation of Jesus, in his resurrection and ascension, is closely related to his moral purity. To offer a suitable sacrifice for sin, Jesus must have been completely sinless. This is proven in Jesus's resurrection. Jesus is a great high priest who obeyed throughout his life, culminating in his death, and was vindicated in his resurrection. For Jesus to be the holy, unblemished, and exalted high priest necessitates that he lived a life of full obedience, even in the face of suffering. Because Jesus has overcome in the days of his flesh (that is, in his estate of humiliation), he is able to serve as a heavenly high priest forever in his estate of glorification.

1–8, 27; Craig R. Koester, *Hebrews: A New Translation with Introduction and Commentary*, AB 36 (New York: Doubleday, 2001), 193; Ellingworth, *Hebrews*, 117–18; David M. Moffitt, *Atonement and the Logic of Resurrection in the Epistle to the Hebrews*, NovTSup 141 (Leiden: Brill, 2011), 53–118.

Conclusion

The good news of the gospel includes the good news of Jesus's high priesthood: because of his final sacrifice, we can be reconciled to God. And Jesus's final sacrifice is the climactic, crowning act of his obedience. The perfection of his obedience is evident both in the finality of his sacrifice and in his resurrection from the dead. Death had no claim on him.

Our consideration of Jesus's obedience as the great high priest leads us to our next chapter, where we will consider in more detail the close relationship between Jesus's perfect obedience and his resurrection. The resurrection is without question one of the key emphases of the Christology of the New Testament. And the resurrection is the proof of Jesus's full obedience. This means that the resurrection emphasis of the New Testament is implicitly an emphasis on the perfect obedience of Jesus. I discuss this further in the following chapter.

7

OBEDIENCE, RESURRECTION, AND SALVATION

I t was a gut-wrenching moment, which baseball fans will discuss as long as the sport endures. In 2010 Detroit Tigers pitcher Armando Galarraga was one out away from making history by pitching an incredibly rare perfect game—a game in which not a single batter reaches base. The twenty-seventh batter hit a ground ball to the right side of the infield. The first baseman ranged to his right, fielded the ball cleanly, and fired the ball on target to Galarraga. The pitcher hustled to cover first base, stepped on the bag just ahead of the runner, and ensured the final out of the game. It was over. With one of baseball's best umpires stationed to make the call at first base, this should have been the climactic ending that sealed the perfect game—with the pitcher himself fittingly recording the final out.

But it wasn't over. Instead, the umpire ruled the runner safe. With no instant replay, the incorrect call stood.

Though Galarraga did what was required for a perfect game, he was not rewarded with the official result. It wasn't a perfect game; it was a near-perfect game.

The aftertaste of what should have been lingers still.

Not everyone who deserves a reward receives it. Nor does everyone who receives a reward deserve it. Sometimes results are unjust.

The resurrection of Jesus is not like that. The resurrection was the crowning vindication of Jesus's perfect obedience.[1] Stated another way, the resurrection was the just verdict of God that Jesus had perfectly conformed to the "do this and live" principle set out in the beginning with Adam and reflected in Leviticus 18:5.[2] Only Jesus has met these demands. In short, if the death of Christ is the climax of his perfect obedience, then the resurrection is the judicial proof and declaration that Jesus's death was unjust and his life of obedience perfectly pleased his Father.

Additionally, Jesus is unique as the God-man. His obedience not only overcomes Adam's disobedience but also provides the answer to divine wrath against human sin. Thus the obedience of Jesus, while focused on his humanity, must also be understood in relation to his divinity. The obedience of Jesus is not the obedience of a private individual, nor is it the obedience of a mere man. The obedience of Jesus is the perfect obedience of a messianic representative, the last Adam. Yet Jesus is also fully God, which means his obedience is qualitatively unique.

1. See especially Geerhardus Vos, *The Pauline Eschatology* (Grand Rapids: Eerdmans, 1961), 151, noted by Richard B. Gaffin Jr., *The Centrality of the Resurrection: A Study in Paul's Soteriology*, Baker Biblical Monographs (Grand Rapids: Baker 1978), 122.

2. See Brandon D. Crowe, *The Last Adam: A Theology of the Obedient Life of Jesus in the Gospels* (Grand Rapids: Baker Academic, 2017), 195.

In this chapter I will look at additional texts that relate the obedience of Jesus to his resurrection, especially from Acts and Paul's Epistles. The resurrection assumes Jesus's perfect obedience. It is the proof that Jesus never sinned and that he entirely, always, fully did the will of God. Since the resurrection is necessary for salvation, this means that Jesus's perfect obedience is necessary for salvation.

The logic of this chapter can thus be summarized simply:

- Jesus's resurrection is necessary for salvation.
- Jesus's resurrection requires his perfect obedience.
- Therefore, Jesus's perfect obedience is necessary for salvation.

Resurrection and Obedience in the Gospels

The Gospels do not devote extended space to the resurrection, but it would be a mistake to think that the resurrection is therefore not important in the Gospels. The resurrection accounts prove that Jesus was right and that his death was not his end. The Gospels' extensive focus on the obedience of Christ and on the rightness of his message is vindicated in Jesus's resurrection. Jesus's resurrection demonstrates the divine, judicial approbation of Jesus's perfect obedience. If the Gospels did not contain resurrection accounts, then the Gospel narratives would be unresolved; the enemies of Jesus would seem to emerge victorious in the spiritual conflict.[3] Jesus would seem to have been silenced, and his repeated predictions of rising from the dead on the third day would have been wrong (e.g., Matt. 12:40; 16:21; 17:23; 26:61; 27:40, 63; Mark 8:31; 9:31; 10:34; 14:58; 15:29; Luke 9:22; 13:32; John 2:19–21; see also Luke 24:7, 46). His enemies would have succeeded in destroying the beloved Son, seizing his inheritance

---

3. See Crowe, *Last Adam*, 193–94.

for themselves (see Mark 12:7). The resurrection accounts are necessary to vindicate the innocence of Jesus—the Holy One of God who had been wrongfully condemned. The new covenant, sealed in Jesus's blood, is effectual because Jesus lives.

In this light, it makes sense that three of the four Gospels (Matthew, Luke, and John) clearly include resurrection appearances of Jesus. The brevity of these accounts belies their weightiness. For example, in Matthew 28:16–20 it is the resurrected Jesus who speaks with all authority in heaven and earth and who commands his disciples to go to all nations. In Luke the risen Jesus explains (twice) how all the Scriptures point to him and blesses his disciples as he ascends into heaven (Luke 24:25–27, 44–47). In John the risen Jesus commands his disciples to receive the Spirit (20:22), restores Peter after his denial of Christ (21:15–19), and probably also commissions his disciples to go to all nations (21:1–13; see also Ezek. 47:1–12). The Gospel of Mark is a bit different, and debate persists about where and how Mark ends. The best option is that Mark ends in 16:8, which means that Mark would be exceptional in not including a resurrection appearance of Jesus. However, this is different than saying Mark's Gospel does not speak about the resurrection. Jesus predicted his resurrection three times in Mark (8:31; 9:31; 10:34), and the angel explicitly tells the women at the tomb that Jesus has been resurrected (16:6–7). Though Mark ends a bit differently and abruptly, it nevertheless ends with the reality of Jesus's resurrection.

The resurrection in the Gospels confirms the perfect obedience of Jesus. It's therefore important that the Gospels end this way. Jesus even speaks of the necessity of his resurrection for salvation (Luke 9:22; 24:7, 26, 46; see also 13:32–33). Yet the Gospels provide little exposition of the resurrection itself. More extended discussion of this crucial event is provided in Acts and Paul's Letters, where it is consistently explained in light of Jesus's obedience.

Resurrection and Obedience in Acts

Jesus says quite a bit about his resurrection in the Gospel of Luke, but we find even more in the Acts of the Apostles— Luke's second volume. In fact, the resurrection of Christ is one of the main points of the entire book of Acts.[4] The resurrection explains how Jesus is both Lord and Christ and how the kingdom of David can last forever. By his resurrection Jesus is also the judge of all people, and in his name forgiveness of sins is offered. Jesus is the forerunner who has overcome death and is characterized by life. He is the Savior. Crucially, all these features of Christology in Acts are tethered to the resurrection of Christ, and the resurrection in Acts is built on the presupposition of the sinlessness of Jesus. Let's now look at this in more detail.

Resurrection and Salvation in Peter's Speeches

The first major speech in Acts is Peter's sermon at Pentecost (2:14–36). In this sermon Peter explains the outpouring of the Holy Spirit that caused the people gathered in Jerusalem to marvel. Yet Peter's focus is on Jesus of Nazareth, the one who had been crucified and had now risen, for it was not possible for Jesus to be held by death (2:24). Jesus is the Holy One of God (2:27; see also Ps. 16:10) who was unjustly sentenced to death (Acts 2:23). Though David expressed confidence that he himself would be delivered as God's anointed, Peter also observed that David remained in the grave. His tomb was well known. Since David was a prophet (2:30), he must have been speaking about the resurrection of the Messiah. This greater son of David—Jesus of Nazareth—did not see decay, for he was more fully the Holy One of God. Jesus was not abandoned

---

4. For what follows see further Brandon D. Crowe, *The Hope of Israel: The Resurrection of Christ in the Acts of the Apostles* (Grand Rapids: Baker Academic, 2020).

to Hades, for he did not belong in Hades. Sin and death had no claim on him. Jesus met the requirements of "do this and live," and he was rewarded with resurrection. Jesus was raised because he was fully committed to doing the will of God, as Paul will explain later in Acts 13.

Jesus's obedience is further assumed at the end of Peter's speech. Repentance is the proper response to the resurrection, that the people's sins might be forgiven (Acts 2:38). Forgiveness comes through Jesus Christ, the sinless one who lives and reigns now as Lord and Christ (2:36). Faith in Christ, the fully obedient and risen King of kings, is the means by which we can be saved.

Peter continues to emphasize the perfect obedience of Christ in Acts 3. When confronting the people after healing a man who was lame, Peter refers to Jesus as the Holy and Righteous One (*ton hagion kai dikaion*, 3:14), who was wrongly condemned to death (see 7:52). He pushes the point further, identifying Jesus as the *archēgos* of life (3:15). As we saw in chapter 6 on Hebrews, *archēgos* is a difficult term to translate (here it can be translated "Author of Life" [ESV, NIV]), but in all four uses in the New Testament it refers to the resurrection of Jesus. It is used twice this way in Acts (3:15; 5:31), where the link with the resurrection is especially clear. In Acts 3:14–15 Peter explains that Jesus is the perfectly holy and righteous one and has authority over life. Death could not hold him. The lame man was healed by faith in the name of Jesus (3:16), and it is to Jesus that all people must listen, heeding the call to repent, that their sins may be blotted out (3:19). For the resurrected Jesus will return and restore all that has been marred by sin (see esp. 3:21). Salvation is offered because Jesus is the resurrected Lord over sin and death.

A similar relationship between Jesus's resurrection, life, and salvation is found in Acts 5. When confronted by the high priest who had forbidden the apostles to teach in the name of Jesus, Peter responded that they must obey God, and they must testify to the resurrection of Jesus. Though Jesus had been unjustly condemned to death, God raised him from the dead (5:29–30). Jesus is the *archēgos* and Savior (5:31). Here again (as in 3:15) *archēgos* communicates Jesus's authority over life. He is also *Savior*—the resurrected one, who is able to grant forgiveness of sins (5:31). Forgiveness and eternal life come through the Holy and Righteous One who was wrongly condemned, but who lives today (see 5:20). Salvation comes not through keeping the law (which no one has been able to keep), but through the grace of the (risen) Lord Jesus (15:10–11).

Eternal life is life in an everlasting kingdom, over which Jesus rules by his resurrection from the dead. He is both Lord and Christ (2:36): the promised Son of David who is also Lord of the whole world (10:36). His obedience secures eternal life.

Resurrection and Salvation in Paul's Speeches

Paul in Acts also relates salvation to the resurrection of Jesus, which is the proof that Jesus was fully devoted to the will of God. This is apparent in Paul's first major speech in Acts at Pisidian Antioch (13:16–41). In this sermon Paul provides a David-focused outline of the history of Israel, showing how Jesus fulfills the promises given to David. In contrast to Saul the Benjaminite, David was a man after God's own heart who did God's will (13:21–22). Yet David's obedience was not complete, and he was not able to deliver an everlasting kingdom, nor provide forgiveness of sins. David's sins were well known, and the kingdom split under his grandson.

David was not the Savior, but the Savior would come from David's line (Acts 13:23). This Savior is Jesus Christ, who was entirely devoted to God's will. This was anticipated by David, but Jesus's obedience excels David's. It's not until verse 30 that Paul explains in more detail *how* Jesus saves his people— especially by being raised from the dead. Like Peter, Paul emphasizes the guiltlessness of Jesus in contrast to the charge leveled against him and the demand that he be put to death (13:28).

The resurrection reversed this sentence of condemnation, which was possible because there was no sin in Jesus. He did not see corruption (13:35–37), for he was fully devoted to God's will as the Holy One of God.

Like Peter, Paul teaches that the risen Jesus reigns over the everlasting kingdom of David (Acts 13:32–34), and he offers forgiveness of sins and justification (13:38–39). To participate in his kingdom is to have eternal life (13:46, 48). Eternal life and forgiveness of sins require the resurrection of Jesus; this means they require Jesus's perfect obedience.

In Acts 17 Paul appears before the Areopagus in Athens, having been accused of preaching foreign divinities (17:18). Paul proclaims that one God rules over all people and that all people must repent. For one righteous man has risen from the dead and will judge righteously on the last day. Salvation is open to all who repent and turn to him. Just as one God created all people, so all people are subject to the man who has risen from the dead. He states that all people trace their origins to Adam (see 17:26), reminding us of the obligation we all owe to God. This obligation is met by the righteous, resurrected Jesus Christ who has authority over all nations. Salvation for all nations comes through him.

Summary: Acts, the Resurrection, and Salvation

In Acts the resurrection of Jesus assumes his entire righteousness and is necessary for forgiveness of sins and eternal life. Because Jesus is the Holy One of God, free from all sin, his body did not see decay. The resurrection of Jesus presupposes his entire obedience and openly vindicates his unjust death. The resurrection proves that Jesus had done all that was necessary to meet the conditions of everlasting life—he was perfectly obedient. The obedience of Christ yields forgiveness of sins and the right to eternal life, which, we have seen, are two benefits of justification.

Geerhardus Vos on the Resurrection of Christ and His Perfect Obedience

"Had something been lacking in the suffering of Christ [i.e., in his passive obedience], then it would have been impossible that the violence of death had ceased even for a moment. Had there been something imperfect in the active obedience of the Mediator, then in no way could an enlivening have taken place in his soul and body. The resurrection must be viewed as God's *de facto* declaration of the perfection of Christ's work in both respects."

—Geerhardus Vos, *Reformed Dogmatics*, ed. and trans. Richard B. Gaffin Jr., 5 vols. (Bellingham, WA: Lexham, 2012–16), 3:221

Acts is distinctive in the extended attention it gives to the resurrection of Jesus in a narrative format, focusing particularly on the speeches of main characters. Jesus is the *archēgos* of life who could not be held by death. He is the perfectly Holy and Righteous One (3:14), who has overcome death and is the Savior of all (5:31; 13:23, 30; 17:30–31). He reigns over an everlasting kingdom and grants forgiveness of sins (e.g., 2:30–36; 13:38–39).

Acts provides one of the most extensive and varied discussions of Jesus's resurrection anywhere in the New Testament. This is especially true when we combine Acts with the Gospel of Luke. Taken together, these two volumes represent over 25 percent of the New Testament and provide a rich reservoir for christological reflection. Salvation comes through Christ, the promised Messiah and last Adam who has risen from the dead. Acts also provides some helpful and necessary background for understanding the New Testament epistles, which were written by some of the characters featured in Acts (Peter, John, James,

Paul, Jude). These epistles often explore the theological rami-
fications of Christ's resurrection more fully. This is especially
true for Paul's Letters, to which we now turn.

Resurrection and Obedience in Paul's Letters

Paul teases out the implications of Jesus's resurrection for
justification extensively. As in Luke, Jesus's resurrection demonstrates his perfect obedience and is necessary for justification. Since I have already covered Romans 5 (see ch. 3), in what
follows I will focus mostly on 1 Corinthians 15 and Philippians
2, both of which relate the resurrection to salvation and the
perfect obedience of Christ.

1 Corinthians 15: Adam, Christ, and the Resurrection

As in Romans 5, in 1 Corinthians 15 Paul relates the person
and work of Christ to the person and work of Adam. For Paul
the resurrection of Christ underscores the necessity for Jesus's
entire obedience for justification. Of first importance for Paul is
not only the death of Christ (15:3) but also that Christ was raised
from the dead (15:4–8). Christ's resurrection is the answer to the
problem of death introduced by Adam's sin. In 15:21 Paul states
the matter succinctly: since by man comes death, by man comes
the resurrection of the dead. Consistent with the argument of
Romans 5, one man's sin led to death for all humanity, whereas
life comes through the second man. In 1 Corinthians 15 Paul
again works with a two-Adam structure to explain both world
history and redemptive history. In 15:45 Paul contrasts the first
man, Adam (*ho prōtos anthrōpos Adam*) with the last Adam
(*ho eschatos Adam*), whom Paul also identifies as the second
man (*ho deuteros anthrōpos*, 15:47)—Jesus Christ. The actions
of two representative men have implications for all humanity.[5]

5. See John Murray, *The Imputation of Adam's Sin* (Grand Rapids: Eerdmans, 1959), 39.

Paul's argument in 1 Corinthians 15 necessitates that Jesus was resurrected as the fully obedient, last Adam. The resurrection was a vindication of his perfect, entire obedience, not *only* the vindication of his unjust death (though it certainly entailed that). The sin that entered the world through Adam was the result of his failure to keep the entire law of God. Christ's resurrection, in contrast, was the result of his doing all that Adam should have done. If Adam's sin consisted in his lack of doing all that was required (personal, entire, exact, and perpetual obedience), Jesus's obedience in his state of humiliation was personal, entire, exact, and perpetual. By this obedience Jesus destroyed the sting of death (15:54–57) and has in principle eradicated death itself (15:25–27). The resurrection victory and authority of Christ are inextricably tied to his perfect obedience in doing what Adam should have done, as illustrated in Paul's quotations of Psalms 8 and 110 (15:25–27), which explain the resurrection authority of Christ in Adamic terms (see Eph. 1:20–23). When Adam sinned, he brought death; when Christ as the last Adam obeyed, he overcame death through his resurrection.

Building on 1 Corinthians 15 (and Rom. 5), Paul's two-Adam paradigm relates to Jesus's obedience and salvation in several ways. Two in particular stand out.

First, the resurrection of Christ was the vindication, or indeed *justification*, of Christ's perfect obedience (passive and active).[6] As Richard Gaffin has trenchantly argued: "The eradication of death in [Christ's] resurrection is nothing less than the removal of the verdict of condemnation and the effective affirmation of his (adamic) righteousness."[7] Gaffin continues, "The enlivening of Christ is judicially declarative not only . . . in connection with his messianic status as son, his adoption,

6. See Turretin, *Inst.*, 14.12.9 (2:440).
7. Gaffin, *Centrality of the Resurrection*, 122.

but also with respect to his (adamic) status as righteous. The constitutive, transforming action of resurrection is specifically forensic in character. It is Christ's justification."[8]

The resurrection as the seal of Jesus's perfect obedience is evident not only from Paul's argument in 1 Corinthians 15 (see 15:17) but also in Romans 1:3–4, where Paul refers to the resurrection as the means by which Jesus was declared Son of God in power. Here again the resurrection highlights the divine approbation of Jesus and his work. The resurrection demonstrates that Jesus was the fully pleasing Son to his Father (see Ps. 2:7 in Acts 13:33). Elsewhere Paul says that Jesus was vindicated by the Spirit (edikaiōthē en pneumati, 1 Tim. 3:16), which refers to the vindication of Jesus's unjust condemnation to death. For Jesus to be raised he must be wholly without sin.

Second, Christ's resurrection is foundational for the justification of those who believe in Christ.[9] In Romans 4:25 Paul explains that Christ has been raised for our justification (ēgerthē dia tēn dikaiōsin hēmōn). Here Paul states that we have been justified because Christ has been raised. Jesus was not handed over for his own sins, but for those of his people. Jesus's perfect obedience led to his victory over sin and death in his resurrection and is foundational for our acceptance before God. The obedience of Christ is assumed in Romans 4, though Paul explains it in more detail in Romans 5.

Paul's argument in Romans 4–5 is consistent with his argument in 1 Corinthians 15. Christ bore our sins in his death—and throughout his life—as a substitute. As the last Adam, Christ acted representatively, and his obedience, manifested in his resurrection from the dead, benefits believers. Whereas sin brings death, the answer to death comes through being united by faith to the resurrected Christ, whose resurrection is the firstfruits of

---

8. Gaffin, *Centrality of the Resurrection*, 124. Gaffin points particularly here to Rom. 4:25; 1 Cor. 15:17; 1 Tim. 3:16.
9. See also Turretin, *Inst.*, 13.17.7 (2:365–66).

a fuller resurrection harvest (1 Cor. 15:20). Christ's resurrection benefits believers no less than Christ's death (see 15:17).[10] Christ's resurrection is the judicial verdict that his obedience was perfect. This means believers' justification is as certain as Christ's resurrection from the dead.

Philippians 2: Obedience Yielding Resurrection Life

Another Pauline text that speaks of the obedience of Jesus in relation to his resurrection is Philippians 2:5–11. Though not as explicit as Romans 5 or 1 Corinthians 15, Philippians 2 may also present the work of Christ in Adamic terms. It is a rich and layered passage that deserves extended reflection. I quote it here for reference:

> [5]Have this mind among yourselves, which is yours in Christ Jesus, [6]who, though he was in the form of God, did not count equality with God a thing to be grasped, [7]but emptied himself, by taking the form of a servant, being born in the likeness of men. [8]And being found in human form, he humbled himself by becoming obedient to the point of death, even death on a cross. [9]Therefore God has highly exalted him and bestowed on him the name that is above every name, [10]so that at the name of Jesus every knee should bow, in heaven and on earth and under the earth, [11]and every tongue confess that Jesus Christ is Lord, to the glory of God the Father.

Notice what Paul says about the obedience of Jesus in Philippians 2:8: "[Christ] humbled himself by becoming obedient to the point of death, even death on a cross." This passage clearly speaks about Christ's death, but Paul does not *only* have Jesus's death in view. Instead, Paul's argument requires that he

---

10. See Gaffin, "The Work of Christ Applied," in *Christian Dogmatics: Reformed Theology for the Church Catholic*, ed. Michael Allen and Scott R. Swain (Grand Rapids: Baker Academic, 2016), 274–86.

is speaking of the entire, perfect obedience of Jesus. At least four reasons support this position.

First, in Philippians 2 Paul mentions not only the death of Christ but also his resurrection/ascension (2:9).[11] As we have seen, Jesus's resurrection is the judicial declaration of Jesus's perfect obedience throughout his life. The resurrection vindicates Jesus's unjust death, but also vindicates his lifelong obedience. The combination of the exaltation of Christ (2:9) with mention of his obedience in 2:8 means that the "obedience unto death" most likely encompasses the totality of Christ's obedience.

Second, the broader context of Paul's argument in Philippians strongly suggests that we should think of the obedience of Christ in Philippians 2:8 broadly. The christological emphasis of Philippians 2:5–11 supports Paul's exhortation to the Philippians to live with one another in love and humility. To support this exhortation, Paul points to the humility of Christ in his state of humiliation (see 2:6–7), which led to his exaltation. This Christlike mindset (2:5) is to be reflected among the Philippians, who should consider others better than themselves (2:3) and look to the interests of others (2:4). A few verses later Paul encourages the Philippians—in light of the full-orbed obedience of Christ—to do *all things* without complaining or disputing (2:14), so that they may be blameless as children of God (2:15).

In light of Paul's call for the Philippians to be obedient in all things, it makes the most sense for Paul to highlight Jesus's obedience throughout his state of humiliation. This obedience was not limited to one or a few acts; Jesus was constantly and in every way obedient.

Third, we must consider what is meant by Jesus's obedience "to the point of death" (*mechri thanatou*) in 2:8. Though this

11. See especially Bavinck, *RD*, 3:434; see also 3:418–19, 423–24, 435. Though they are separate events, the resurrection and ascension can be together under the rubric of Christ's estate of exaltation; see Bavinck, *RD*, 3:339.

sounds like Paul is speaking only of Jesus's death, his argument renders it extremely likely that in 2:8 he is speaking of Jesus's obedience more broadly rather than speaking *only* of his death. Paul refers to Jesus's entire, lifelong obedience, which includes most climactically his death.

Support for this comes in the flexibility of *mechri* ("unto" or "to the point of") in Paul's writings, which often appears to be used *inclusively* rather than *exclusively*. In other words, the term includes that which precedes the terminus to which it leads. For example, we find the phrase *mechri thanatou* ("to the point of death") again in Philippians 2:30, there in reference to Epaphroditus's willingness to minister even to the point of death. To be sure, Paul seems to emphasize here the terminus, or the extent, to which Epaphroditus was willing to go—he was willing to serve *even to the point of death*.[12] At the same time, Epaphroditus did not actually die in the service that Paul describes. Thus, Epaphroditus's ministry included his willingness to sacrifice his own life, but *mechri thanatou* must include all he did to serve the Philippians, *short of* his own death. Epaphroditus's willingness to sacrifice his own life follows the pattern of Christ, yet the same could be said of his entire ministry of service and suffering. If so, it's likely that Paul's earlier statement about Christ's obedience in 2:8 should likewise be taken to refer to Jesus's life of service as well. Thus "becoming obedient to the point of death" in 2:8 probably includes more than *only* the obedience of Jesus in his death (though 2:8b confirms that Jesus's death on a cross is indeed squarely in view).

Paul focuses on the death of Christ in Philippians 2:8, but not on his death as an isolated event. Jesus's death incorporates, sums up, and completes the obedience of his entire life.[13] Jesus

---

12. The phrasing is slightly different for Epaphroditus than for Christ, for Epaphroditus *approached* (*ēngisen*) the point of death (*mechri thanatou*).

13. Again reflecting the language of Bavinck, *RD*, 3:378; see also 3:385, 407–8. See also Turretin, *Inst.*, 14.13.18 (2:450–51).

persevered in obedience throughout his life—he never grumbled, never selfishly disputed, and always considered others better than himself (see 2:3–4, 14). In the death of Christ we see most clearly what is always true of Jesus's obedience: the passive and the active are inextricably bound together.[14] Other Pauline uses of *mechri* seem to corroborate this inclusive interpretation of *mechri* (see Rom. 5:14; 15:19; Gal. 4:19; Eph. 4:13; 1 Tim. 6:14; 2 Tim. 2:9).

In light of these texts, *mechri* in Philippians 2:8 most likely has in view Jesus's entire life, and not only the terminus point of his death. Yet, even if *mechri* does focus only on Jesus's death, the context of Philippians 2 necessitates that Jesus's death would still serve synecdochically for Jesus's entire, unified obedience—that is, it's the part that represents the whole.[15] And even if Paul intends only the death of Christ, this would still highlight both Christ's passive and active obedience, since these are logical rather than temporal distinctions.

Fourth, Paul's discussion in Philippians 3:9 of the righteousness of God that comes through faith supports the argument that Christ's entire obedience is in view in Philippians 2. I argued in chapter 2 that the righteousness of Christ for justification is the righteousness of his entire obedience.[16] In light of this, the righteousness of God that comes through faith must be a christological righteousness that benefits those who believe in Christ. The contrast Paul makes, in other words, is between one's own righteousness (which is insufficient) and the salvific righteousness of Christ that comes by faith. Only the righteousness of Christ's entire obedience suffices for justification.

One final observation from Philippians 3 is relevant as well. In this context Paul speaks of an eschatological goal—attaining

---

14. So also Donald Macleod, *Christ Crucified: Understanding the Atonement* (Downers Grove, IL: InterVarsity, 2014), 180.

15. Bavinck, *RD*, 3:378.

16. This point is made by John Murray, *Redemption Accomplished and Applied* (Grand Rapids: Eerdmans, 1955), 123–24.

the resurrection of the dead (3:11–12). As I have shown in this chapter, resurrection life is contingent upon the perfect obedience of Christ. If Paul (or anyone) is to meet the covenantal requirements for resurrection life, then he must trust in Christ, who alone embodied perfect obedience leading to his resurrection. Attaining the resurrection of the dead can thus only be realized in the context of union with Christ.

Summary: Paul, the Resurrection, and Salvation

Paul explores the salvific implications of Christ's resurrection more fully than any other New Testament author. Jesus was justified in his resurrection, and the justification of believers is contingent upon his resurrection. Christ's resurrection also highlights the eschatological nature of justification: justification is an eschatological reality in which believers are declared righteous by faith in the present age, prior to the final judgment. What was true for Christ is true for those united to Christ by faith—freedom from sin and death and the promise of new life. Paul's emphasis on Christ's resurrection necessitates the entire obedience of Jesus, for otherwise Jesus would not have been raised from the dead. And since the resurrection is necessary for salvation, the perfect obedience of Jesus is necessary for salvation.

Coda: The Obedience of the *Divine* Son of God

As we approach the conclusion of this chapter, we near the end of the discussion of Jesus's obedience. In the next two chapters I will discuss the *implications* of Jesus's obedience in more detail, especially in relation to justification and sanctification. Before we do so, it is crucial to discuss one further aspect of the obedience of Jesus that I have not discussed in any detail—the relationship of Jesus's obedience as a man to his divinity. The representative obedience of Christ must not be understood *only* as the perfect obedience owed by humanity to God. Since Jesus is the God-man, his obedience is also a *divine* work. If we don't understand this, then our understanding of the obedience of Christ will not be sufficient.

Considering Jesus's divinity requires us to consider the nature of Christology—one of the most important, but difficult, issues of Christian theology. In what follows I discuss briefly three points related to the divinity of Christ as it pertains to his representative, salvific obedience. First, I show that Jesus as Mediator is the unique God-man, and he acts as mediator according to both his human nature and divine nature. Second, I explain why it's necessary for the work of salvation to be a divine work. Third, I relate the divinity of Christ and his perfect work to the resurrection.

One Mediator, Two Natures

First, the one Mediator is Jesus Christ. He is one person (the Son of God), who is eternal and divine. In his incarnation this one, divine person took to himself a human nature. Now this one, divine person has two natures: divine and human. As Mediator, Jesus acts according to both natures. But it is always the *person* (the Son of God) who acts. This means that Jesus's obedience is always the obedience of the God-man. If we neglect this important reality, we will not properly understand the obedience of Christ.

Throughout this study I have assumed Jesus's humanity in his obedience to the law and his suffering on behalf of sin. Yet this is by no means the whole story, for Jesus is also divine. It is not my aim in this study to defend the divinity of Jesus. The divinity of Christ has been the orthodox Christian position from the earliest days of the church,[17] which reflects the teach-

17. See the "rule of faith" (*regula fidei*) in the early church, which is closely reflected in the Apostles' Creed. For examples, see Everett Ferguson, *The Rule of Faith: A Guide*, Cascade Companions (Eugene, OR: Cascade Books, 2015), 1–15.

ing of the New Testament.[18] The human nature of Jesus and the divine nature of Jesus are united—yet remain distinct—in one person. Jesus is the only Mediator between God and man (1 Tim. 2:5) and is unique as the one who is both God and man. He is *theanthrōpos*—the God-man.

Many discussions of the work of Christ focus on his humanity, while downplaying or ignoring his divinity. Regardless of why this may be, one point needs to be made clearly: the divinity of Jesus is a nonnegotiable matter for orthodox Christianity. And as I will argue in the next section, if Jesus were not divine, then his work would not be effective unto salvation.

Mediatorial Obedience as a Divine Work

Second, we must speak carefully about the relationship between the divine and human natures. They are not mixed or confused, but are united in one person. As Mediator, Jesus, the Son of God, acts according to both natures. In other words, the Son's incarnate, mediatorial actions are not simply human actions, nor are they simply divine actions; they are the actions of the God-man—the incarnate Son of God.[19] This means the Son's earthly obedience as mediator is not *simply* human obedience, but is at every moment the obedience of the God-man.

The need for *human* obedience should be fairly clear by this point in the book. As a man, Jesus had to obey where Adam failed. He fulfilled the covenant of works "as a way to eternal life for himself and his own."[20] Further, since by man comes

---

18. E.g., John 1:1, 18; 1 Cor. 8:5–6; Phil. 2:5–11; Col. 1:13–20; Titus 2:13; Heb. 1:3; 2 Pet. 1:1; 1 John 5:20; many others.

19. See John Owen, ΧΡΙΣΤΟΛΟΓΙΑ: *Or, A Declaration of the Glorious Mystery of the Person of Christ*, in *The Glory of Christ*, vol. 1 of *The Works of John Owen*, ed. William H. Goold (Edinburgh: Banner of Truth, 1965), 228–35; Turretin, *Inst.*, 12.2.11 (2:176–77); 14.2 (2:379–84); Vos, *Reformed Dogmatics*, 3:50–51; see also WLC, questions and answers 38–39.

20. Bavinck, *RD*, 3:379; see also Owen, ΧΡΙΣΤΟΛΟΓΙΑ, 178–205; Vos, *Reformed Dogmatics*, 3:2.

death, it's necessary that by a man comes the resurrection of the dead (1 Cor. 15:21).

But this is not the whole story. For, if Jesus was *only* a man, he would not be able to accomplish salvation. His obedience must be the obedience of the God-man. Though this deserves (and has received) extended reflection, I list three interrelated reasons here.

1. As redeemer, Jesus must be the God-man in order to be free from original sin. If Jesus were born by natural procreation, he would have been implicated in the sin of Adam, and thus unable to save humanity from sin.[21] In other words, were the divine Son of God to have been descended from Adam through an ordinary birth, he would have been represented by sinful Adam in the covenant of works, and would thus have been under condemnation.[22] The virginal conception of Jesus points to his true humanity, and also to his holiness as the Son of God.[23] He is the God-man.

2. It is also necessary that the mediator be divine in order to appease the wrath of God against sin.[24] Only the God-man could do this.[25] For as we have seen, the penalty for human sin must be paid by a human. Yet no mere human is able to withstand the wrath of God. But Jesus can, as evidenced by his resurrection (see the next section). As Geerhardus Vos notes, "The suffering and all the active obedience, although accomplished in [the Son of God's] humanity, was nevertheless divine suffering and divine obedience—that is, of infinite value."[26] As this

21. See Turretin, *Inst.*, 13.11 (2:340–47); Vos, *Reformed Dogmatics*, 3:47.
22. See, e.g., Vos, *Reformed Dogmatics*, 3:22, 25.
23. See Amandus Polanus von Polansdorf, *Syntagma Theologiae Christianae* (Hanover: Wechel, 1615), §6.14 (pp. 365–66).
24. See, e.g., HC, questions and answers 14–15, 17; WLC, question and answer 38; Petrus van Mastricht, *Theoretical-Practical Theology*, trans. Todd M. Rester, ed. Joel R. Beeke, 7 vols. (Grand Rapids: Reformation Heritage, 2018–), 2:515.
25. See, e.g., Bavinck, *RD*, 3:345; Louis Berkhof, *Systematic Theology*, 4th ed. (Grand Rapids: Eerdmans, 1996), 319; Vos, *Reformed Dogmatics*, 3:48.
26. Vos, *Reformed Dogmatics*, 3:24.

quote indicates, this also means that the work of the Mediator must be infinitely valuable.[27]

3. Finally, Christ's obedience as Mediator benefits others. This also points to his divinity.[28] The Mediator who accomplishes salvation is the Mediator who applies salvation.[29]

Resurrection of the Mediator

Third, Jesus's divinity is also apparent in his resurrection from the dead. This follows from the infinite value and wrath-bearing nature of Jesus's obedience and sacrifice. Jesus was not kept in the grave, for his work was sufficient and pleasing to God. This assumes his divinity, which enabled his humanity to withstand the wrath of God.[30]

But in addition, the resurrection points to the divinity of Jesus because only God can grant new life (see Deut. 32:39). Though many texts speak of Jesus being passively raised from the dead, he also speaks of raising himself from the dead (see John 10:17–18).[31] Turretin again captures the matter memorably (and polemically):

> It is absurd and ridiculous that a mere man . . . who has died, should raise himself from the dead. But that the God-man (*theanthrōpon*) should raise up his humanity by virtue of his divine power is so far from being absurd that to deny it is blasphemous and wicked.[32]

---

27. E.g., Vos, *Reformed Dogmatics*, 3:48; Berkhof, *Systematic Theology*, 319; Charles Hodge, *Systematic Theology*, 3 vols. (1872–73; repr., Peabody, MA: Hendrickson, 2008), 2:395; Turretin, *Inst.*, 13.3.20 (2:303); Canons of Dort 2.3.

28. Vos, *Reformed Dogmatics*, 3:21–22.

29. Turretin, *Inst.*, 13.3.19 (2:302); Berkhof, *Systematic Theology*, 319; Gaffin, "Work of Christ Applied," 269–70.

30. See Vos, *Reformed Dogmatics*, 3:24.

31. Turretin (*Inst.*, 13.17.7 [2:365–66]) argues that God (the Father) is often said to raise Jesus in order to highlight the full satisfaction made by Christ for our sins (see Rom. 4:25).

32. Turretin, *Inst.*, 13.17.8 (2:366).

The resurrection demonstrates not only the perfection of Jesus's obedient life but also his divinity.

In sum, "the reason why Christ had to be God and man in one person was so that a salvation could be achieved that could truly benefit us."[33] The obedience of the divine Son of God is necessary to free us from sin and the wrath of God and raise us to eternal life. Francis Turretin presses home this point precisely and poetically:

> The work of redemption could not have been performed except by a God-man (*theanthrōpon*) associating by incarnation the human nature with the divine by an indissoluble bond. For since to redeem us, two things were most especially required—the acquisition of salvation and the application of [salvation]; the endurance of death for satisfaction and victory over [death] for the enjoyment of life—our mediator ought to be God-man (*theanthrōpos*) to accomplish these things:

man to suffer	God to overcome
man to receive the punishment we deserved	God to endure and drink it to the dregs
man to acquire salvation for us by dying	God to apply it to us by overcoming
man to become ours by the assumption of flesh	God to make us like himself by the bestowal of the Spirit

> This neither a mere man nor God alone could do. For neither could God alone be subject to death, nor could man alone conquer it. Man alone could die for men; God alone could vanquish death.[34]

---

33. Vos, *Reformed Dogmatics*, 3:63.
34. Turretin, *Inst.*, 13.3.19 (2:302–3). I have reformatted the quote for clarity.

Conclusion: Obedience, the Resurrection, and Salvation

The New Testament's emphasis on the resurrection is a message about salvation, and it is a message about the unique obedience of Jesus Christ our Savior.[35]

Tragically, many people have been unjustly murdered or sentenced to death. Uriah was a righteous man who was betrayed by David and died in battle for God's kingdom. Stephen was a godly man wrongly condemned to death by a mob. In early Christian tradition, both Peter and Paul were sentenced to death and executed. Many others have died unjustly by the hands of others—from Abel to Zechariah. Yet none of these were sufficiently holy to rise from the dead; nor were any inherently able to raise themselves to new life. To overcome death, all were dependent on a work outside of themselves.

Only one person has been unjustly sentenced to death and overcome this condemnation on the basis of his own work. Jesus's resurrection from the dead proves not only that his sentence of condemnation was unjust but that he did *nothing* deserving death; his obedience yielded life. And at every point his obedience was the work of the God-man, seen preeminently in his resurrection to new life.

The resurrection proves the perfect obedience of Jesus and is also the guarantee that all who believe in Jesus will one day rise. For Jesus himself is the resurrection and the life (John 11:25). The general resurrection of God's people to eternal life is contingent upon the unique resurrection of Jesus, predicated on his perfect obedience as the God-man.

---

35. See HC, question and answer 45.

PART 3

IMPLICATIONS

8

JESUS'S OBEDIENCE AND OUR JUSTIFICATION

E arn it."

Those were the dying words of Captain John Miller, Tom Hanks's character in *Saving Private Ryan*. Miller and his men had trudged through World War II battle zones across France looking for Private James Ryan in order to send him home from the front lines. In the end, Miller and many others gave their lives so that Ryan might live.

At the end of the movie the aged James Ryan visits John Miller's grave, accompanied by his family. Ryan tells Miller's gravestone that he has done his best to earn what was given him by living the best life he could. He then turns to his wife and asks her if he's led a good life. Has he been a good man? Has he lived a life worthy of the sacrifice made for him? How could he ever repay such a debt?

The sacrifices made by John Miller on behalf of James Ryan are a powerful picture of the sacrificial love of Christ who gave his life that his people might live. We would have felt differently if the aged Ryan had cursed and spit on Miller's grave. Instead, we empathize with Ryan's trek to Normandy and understand that he has done his best to live a worthy life.

If it is important to live worthily in light of a sacrifice made in war, the importance is heightened when we consider the sacrifice of the eternal Son of God for the salvation of sinners. Maybe we're even reminded of those final words of Captain Miller: "Earn it."

On one hand, the New Testament makes it clear that it is by grace that we are saved, and there is nothing we can do to earn salvation (Eph. 2:8–9). And yet Christians are called to true obedience (2:10), to live a life worthy of the gospel (Phil. 1:27). We wouldn't say we "earn" our salvation, but is there any sense in which we are required to live worthily of the sacrifice made for us? Is there a sense in which our works do, in some way, aid our acceptance before God? Do our works somehow help secure our final salvation? And if our obedience is necessary, how does this relate to the unique work of Christ? Is it possible to claim the work of Christ by faith and reject the call to obedience? These are important questions, and they have received a variety of answers. In this chapter and the following chapter I relate these issues to the need for Jesus's perfect obedience.

To put the matter simply, the question I will address in the next two chapters is, How does our obedience relate to Christ's obedience? If Jesus is the perfectly obedient Savior, and if his perfect obedience is necessary for salvation, then what is the role of our works? How important are they?

Two Grave Errors

Insufficient answers to such questions have led to two categories of errors. On the one hand, there is the danger of sinful living—antinomianism. This approach says that if we are saved by grace, then what we do doesn't matter. We can live as we please without negative consequences. On the other hand, there is the danger of legalism: saying that our works somehow add to what Christ has done and are part of the equation of our acceptance before God.[1] Antinomianism ostensibly seems the best way to preserve free grace. But it fails to take seriously enough the calls to obedience in Scripture. Legalism ostensibly upholds the call to obedience but in the end undermines the work of Christ by positing that our own works somehow supplement or add to the work of Christ.

Both these approaches are inadequate, and yet in their most sincere forms, they want to preserve two important truths: the free grace of Christ on the one hand *and* the call to Christian obedience on the other. Navigating these theological waters is tricky, and the current is often deceptively strong, pulling us to one side or the other. In contrast to antinomianism, our works really do matter, even though they are not the foundation of our acceptance before God. In contrast to legalism, we really can't save ourselves by anything we can do. Only *perfect* obedience can suffice for eternal life, and our works are not perfect.

Two Key Terms

Navigating these theological waters requires an understanding of the traditional theological categories of *justification* and *sanctification*. These are closely related, but distinct, and help us correlate the unique work of Christ to our own works. These categories are well established in the Reformed tradition, and they best do justice to the various facets of many biblical texts.

1. See Sinclair B. Ferguson, *The Whole Christ: Legalism, Antinomianism, and Gospel Assurance—Why the Marrow Controversy Still Matters* (Wheaton: Crossway, 2016).

The outline for the present chapter is as follows: First, I introduce two key concepts: justification and sanctification. Second, I explore biblical teaching on justification and how this relates to Jesus's perfect obedience and our imperfect obedience. Only Jesus's perfect obedience suffices for justification.

Building on this, in chapter 9 I explore the biblical teaching on sanctification and how this relates to Jesus's perfect obedience and our imperfect obedience. Though our obedience is imperfect and is not the foundation of justification, it *is* necessary for salvation. Understanding what this does and does not mean is crucial. In chapter 9 I also sketch some practical implications that arise from a proper understanding of the relationship between justification and sanctification. In light of the perfect obedience of Christ, how then ought we to live?

Distinguishing Justification and Sanctification

In chapter 2 I introduced two key terms: justification and sanctification. I argued that justification is an act of God's grace whereby sinners are forgiven and counted righteous in his sight on the basis of Christ's perfect obedience, and these benefits come by faith alone. Justification is therefore best understood as the way that a holy God makes sinners acceptable in his sight, and the ground of justification is the perfect obedience of Jesus Christ.

Sanctification is closely related, but is different. Sanctification can be understood from various angles. For example, sanctification can be used to refer to a once-for-all, definitive action in which a person is set apart as holy to God. This is an important facet of sanctification, but I will use the term primarily to refer to the process of growth in holiness.

Understanding justification and sanctification properly is necessary to do justice to both (1) the uniqueness and necessity of Christ's perfect work for salvation and (2) the biblical emphasis on the need for our perseverance in obedience. On the one hand, our works are in no way the foundation of our justification. I have already argued this. Justification is about what God does for us on the basis of Christ's perfect obedience. On the other hand, I will argue in chapter 9 that our good works are necessary for final salvation. But—crucially—our works must not be construed as the foundation of our justification. Instead, they are the *fruit* of true faith. Precise, technical language is necessary to construe these properly. Thankfully, previous generations of biblical interpreters have provided a wealth of nuance on these issues; we don't need to reinvent the wheel.

I quoted the Westminster Shorter Catechism definition of justification in chapter 2. It will be helpful to compare this with the definition of sanctification in the Westminster Shorter Catechism. I include both definitions here, for comparison:

Comparing Justification and Sanctification: Westminster Shorter Catechism 33 and 35 (1647)*

Q 33. What is justification?	Q 35. What is sanctification?
A 33. Justification is an **act** of God's free grace, wherein he pardons all our sins, and accepts us as righteous in his sight, only for the righteousness of Christ imputed to us, and received by faith alone.	A 35. Sanctification is the **work** of God's free grace, whereby we are renewed in the whole man after the image of God, and are enabled more and more to die unto sin, and live unto righteousness.

*Edited for style and emphasis added.

Both justification and sanctification are attributed to the grace of God, and both are by faith.[2] Both find their context in union with Christ. Both justification and sanctification are necessary for final salvation. Yet, as I argued in chapter 2, whereas justification is a unilateral, forensic *act* of God, sanctification is a *work* of God—a process of growth. Justification is a onetime declaration, which needs no improvement; sanctification is an ongoing process that is always imperfect in this life. Christ's righteousness is *imputed* in justification; Christ's righteousness is *infused* in sanctification.[3] Thus, in justification our righteousness is entirely that of another—it is perfect; in sanctification we grow more and more into the image of Christ, though always imperfectly in this age. Justification is accomplished by God apart from any work of the sinner, whereas growth in sanctification requires the activity of the believer.[4]

Both justification and sanctification must also be understood properly in relation to the perfect obedience of Jesus Christ. In justification, the perfect obedience of Jesus—his righteousness—is imputed to believers by faith alone. In sanctification those who are justified are conformed more and more to the image of Christ. In both respects Christ is central.

Justification, Jesus's Obedience, and Our Obedience

The Logic of Imputation

One of the most debated aspects of justification is the notion of Christ's righteousness. What is it? And how does it relate to

2. Geerhardus Vos, *Reformed Dogmatics*, ed. and trans. Richard B. Gaffin Jr., 5 vols. (Bellingham, WA: Lexham, 2012–16), 4:202.

3. E.g., Bavinck, *RD*, 4:248–52; Turretin, *Inst.*, 16.3.6 (2:647); 16.8.24 (2:682); 17.1.3 (2:689); see also David B. Garner, *Sons in the Son: The Riches and Reach of Adoption in Christ* (Phillipsburg, NJ: P&R, 2016), 240–49.

4. See Bavinck, *RD*, 4:252–56.

Herman Bavinck on Justification and Sanctification in Christ

"Justification and sanctification, accordingly, grant the same benefits, rather, the entire Christ; they only differ in the manner in which they grant him. In justification, Christ is granted to us juridically, in sanctification, ethically; by the former we become the righteousness of God in him; by the latter he himself comes to dwell in us by his Spirit and renews us after his image."

— Herman Bavinck, *RD*, 4:249

us? I argued in chapter 2 that Jesus's righteousness is *imputed* to believers in justification. This concept has often been challenged. Yet it remains important, for imputation is tightly tethered to Jesus's perfect obedience. Because Jesus is a representative, his actions can benefit others. And since Jesus is the only perfectly obedient one, only his obedience suffices to meet the demands of a perfectly holy God.

By this point I have argued at length that Jesus is the perfectly obedient Savior. I have said less about human sinfulness, but Scripture is clear that all people are sinners. All have sinned and fall short of the glory of God. Paul states this explicitly in Romans 3:23, and to this we could add an abundance of other scriptural texts.[5]

To meet the demands of eternal life the imperfection of human works must be overcome by the perfect obedience of the God-man, whose righteousness meets the demands of God and who can bear the wrath of God. This is a crucial point: *sinful, human works—even sincere, regenerate works—can never meet*

5. E.g., Gen. 6:5; Ps. 51:5; Rom. 6:23; Eph. 2:1; James 2:10; 3:2.

the demands for eternal life.[6] Our works can never meet the requirement for justification. This means that the righteousness that is counted for sinners in justification is *in no way* our own righteousness, which would wilt under the judgment of God. It must remain the legal righteousness of the representatively obedient one, Jesus Christ. His righteousness counts for us and stands up to the justice of God.

One objection lodged against the imputation of Christ's righteousness in justification is the misunderstanding that this refers to the imputation of God's own, divine righteousness. Yet we must nuance this appropriately. The best articulations of imputation doctrine recognize that we are speaking specifically of the righteousness of Christ—that is, of his obedience as Mediator. Turretin deals decisively with the nature of righteousness that is imputed:

> By the righteousness of Christ we do not understand here the "essential righteousness of God" dwelling in us. . . . That righteousness could not be communicated to us subjectively and formally which is an essential attribute of God without our becoming gods also. And the Scripture everywhere refers *the righteousness of Christ*, which is imputed to us, to *the obedience of his life and the suffering of his death*, by which he answered the demands of the law and perfectly fulfilled it. . . . If Christ is [Yahweh], our righteousness, and if he is made to us righteousness by the Father, this is not said with respect to essential righteousness, but to *the obedience which is imputed to us for righteousness*. This is called the righteousness of God because it belongs to a divine person and so is of infinite value and is highly pleasing and acceptable to God. *By this righteousness then, we understand the entire*

6. E.g., Turretin, *Inst.*, 16.2–3 (2:637–56); see also 17.5.16, 18–19 (2:715–16); Bavinck, *RD*, 4:209–14; Canons of Dort 2, error 4; Charles Hodge, *Systematic Theology*, 3 vols. (1872–73; repr., Peabody, MA: Hendrickson, 2008), 3:138–39.

Francis Turretin on the Righteousness of Christ

"Therefore when we say that the righteousness of Christ is imputed to us for justification and that we are just before God through imputed righteousness and not through any righteousness inherent in us, we mean nothing else than that the obedience of Christ rendered in our name to God the Father is so given to us by God that it is reckoned to be truly ours and that it is the sole and only righteousness on account of and by the merit of which we are absolved from the guilt of our sins and obtain a right to life; and that there is in us no righteousness or good works by which we can deserve such great benefits which can bear the severe examination of the divine court, if God willed to deal with us according to the rigor of his law; that we can oppose nothing to it except the merit and satisfaction of Christ, in which alone, terrified by the consciousness of sin, we can find a safe refuge against the divine wrath and peace for our souls."

—Francis Turretin, *Inst.*, 16.3.9 (2:648)

---

obedience of Christ—of his life as well as of his death, active as well as passive.[7]

In other words, the righteousness of imputation is the entire, perfect obedience of Jesus Christ, though this righteousness is indeed closely related to God's own righteousness in Christ

---

7. Turretin, *Inst.*, 16.3.14 (2:650–51), edited for style; emphasis added. See also Bavinck, *The Wonderful Works of God: Instruction in the Christian Religion according to the Reformed Confession*, trans. Henry Zylstra (repr., Philadelphia: Westminster Seminary Press, 2019), 434.

155

(see 1 Cor. 1:30; Phil. 3:9).[8] And since Christ is the God-man, his righteousness is the righteousness of God.[9]

Imputation and Forensic Justification

If justification is based on the perfect obedience of Jesus Christ alone, then justification must be declarative and forensic, not transformative.[10] Put differently, justification is a legal declaration that sinners are in a right standing before God, and this apart from any work of the sinner. As I discussed in chapter 2, this is what it means for justification to be forensic. In contrast, a transformative view of justification states that sinners are *infused* with righteousness that enables them, in some sense, to meet God's requirements for justification.

On a forensic understanding of justification, the righteousness on which one stands before God is entirely the righteousness of Jesus Christ. On a transformative understanding of justification, the righteousness of the sinner becomes, by the grace of God, part of the equation for the way one meets God's standards for acceptance before him. This remains true even if someone ventured to argue that righteousness is *both* infused *and* imputed in justification; in this case, the infusion of righteousness means that our obedience in some way factors into justification.

Here again it's important to understand God's requirements for justification. Put differently, what does God require for eternal life? If the answer is perfect obedience, then the imperfect—though sincere—obedience of believers can never meet this demand. Transformative justification fails to convince. Though I agree that good works are necessary, which proponents of

8. G. K. Beale, *A New Testament Biblical Theology: The Unfolding of the Old Testament in the New* (Grand Rapids: Baker Academic, 2011), 471–74.

9. See Hodge, *Systematic Theology*, 3:143–44.

10. See further Turretin, *Inst.*, 16.1 (2:633–36); 16.7.14 (2:672–73); Hodge, *Systematic Theology*, 3:144–45.

> ## Heidelberg Catechism (1563), Question and Answer 62
>
> **Q.** Why can't the good we do make us right with God, or at least help make us right with him?
>
> **A.** Because the righteousness which can pass God's scrutiny must be entirely perfect and must in every way measure up to the divine law. Even the very best we do in this life is imperfect and stained with sin.

transformative justification often seek to highlight, the good works of sinners can never be the foundation of their acceptance before God. One's own good works—even regenerate good works—can never be the ground for justification. Turretin again argues persuasively that it would be a contradiction to say that we are justified by inherent righteousness *and* by the forgiveness of sins; we must either be justified by our own works or by the works of another.[11] There is no middle ground.

This debate was at the heart of the Reformation. Forensic justification has been codified in many Protestant creeds, whereas transformative justification was codified in the Council of Trent (1564) as the position of the Roman Catholic Church. The Council of Trent included believers' good works as contributing to their justification and pronounced a curse on all who teach justification by faith alone.[12] This issue has historically

11. Turretin, *Inst.*, 16.2.14 (2:643).
12. Council of Trent, session 6, "Canons concerning Justification, 13 January 1547," in *Decrees of the Ecumenical Councils: Trent to Vatican II*, ed. Norman P. Tanner, vol. 2 (Washington, DC: Georgetown University Press, 1990), ch. 7 (pp. 673–74), canons 9, 11–12 (p. 679). See also Bavinck, *RD*, 4:204–9; Leonardo De Chirico, "Not by Faith Alone? An Analysis of the Roman Catholic Doctrine of Justification from Trent to the *Joint Declaration*," in *The Doctrine on Which*

been a fault line, and understandably so. This also explains much of the pushback from Protestants—especially Protestants in the Reformed tradition—against contemporary arguments that include our works as part of the equation of justification, such as the popular refrain that we are justified "based on the whole life lived." This phrasing presents a view of justification that is—or at least appears to be close to—a transformative view of justification that includes our works. This is not mere semantics; this approach muddies the biblical focus on and need for Christ's perfect, unique obedience. This moves the confidence away from Christ's certain work to an uncertain trust in our own works.

To be sure, good works are required for the person who is justified, but this is different than saying our good works somehow contribute to our justification.[13] The basis of justification is the perfect righteousness of Jesus Christ. Further, if the righteousness of Christ is imputed to believers and is the ground of their justification, this means justification is forensic and decisive, for no one can add any value to the perfect obedience of Jesus Christ. God's actions on behalf of sinners in justification must not be confused with any moral action of the believer.[14] The believer's obedience must therefore be understood differently from the obedience that counts for justification.

Faith and Union with Christ

To speak about justification is also to speak about faith. In the Protestant-Reformation tradition, justification comes *by* faith *alone*—apart from any work sinners can contribute. This is consistent with what I've already argued—namely, that imperfect obedience cannot meet the demands for justification

---

the *Church Stands or Falls: Justification in Biblical, Theological, Historical, and Pastoral Perspective*, ed. Matthew Barrett (Wheaton: Crossway, 2019), 737–42.

13. I am paraphrasing Turretin, *Inst.*, 16.8.13 (2:680).

14. Turretin, *Inst.*, 16.2.24 (2:645).

and eternal life, which requires perfect obedience. Put simply, faith is the means by which the righteousness of Christ benefits us. Faith adds nothing to the perfect work of Christ—indeed, it cannot!—but rests on Christ alone for salvation.

Justification is by faith alone because the righteousness on which our justification hinges is entirely the righteousness of the perfect obedience of Jesus Christ. I want to highlight three things about this traditional emphasis on faith alone, which best accord with the New Testament's emphasis on the perfect, representative obedience of Christ. First, we need to understand faith not as a work, but as an *instrument*. Second, we need to understand the object of saving faith—our faith is *in Christ*. Third, we need to understand the centrality of union with Christ by faith.

1. Faith as Instrument

First, it's important to emphasize that faith is not a *work* by which we are justified. This is a common misunderstanding. I have even heard it said that faith is the one work we can do. Perhaps this draws upon John 6:29 ("Jesus answered them, 'This is the work of God, that you believe in him whom he has sent'"), but this view will not hold up to scrutiny. Faith—even true, saving faith—remains imperfect, which means that even if faith *were* a work, then it would not meet the demands of God's justice and would be insufficient to secure eternal life. Since eternal life must be gained by the perfect work of Christ, faith is the *means by which* sinners benefit from the perfect work of Christ. Nothing a sinner can do—not even faith—can secure, or help secure, justification. We saw earlier that John 6:29 is an ironic statement, since believing is, strictly speaking, no work at all.[15]

---

15. See also Turretin, *Inst.*, 16.7.22 (2:674–75); Bavinck, *RD*, 3:498, 4:222; Bavinck, *Reformed Ethics: Created, Fallen, and Converted Humanity*, ed. John Bolt, 3 vols. (Grand Rapids: Baker Academic, 2019–), 1:267–70.

Faith is thus not a work but an *instrument*; faith is the *means by which* the perfect obedience of Christ can be counted to sinners for salvation.[16] Put simply, faith is the instrument of justification. Precision is necessary here. Faith is not the *basis* on which we are saved; that basis is the perfect obedience of Christ. We are thus not saved *on the basis of faith*, but we are saved *through* faith (see Eph. 2:8). True faith does not make one somehow worthy of salvation, nor is faith a work, properly speaking.

This understanding of faith as an instrument best accords with the focus on the unique obedience of Jesus. If Jesus's obedience is sufficient, then there is nothing we can add to it. Faith is thus the means by which we benefit from it, as Christ with his benefits is applied to us by the Holy Spirit; faith adds nothing to the work of Christ.

Historically, many who have defined faith as a work—such as the Socinians—often also downplayed the substitutionary life and death of Christ.[17] The Socinian position—seen, for example, in the Racovian Catechism—is that we are saved by our faithfulness and perseverance in obedience.[18] Thus, faith is a work. This position, while misguided, was nevertheless consistent within its own framework: if Jesus has not fully made satisfaction (and indeed, if he is not fully divine), then there remains something for us to add. But if Christ has perfectly obeyed and died as a representative, our faith must not be construed as a *work* lest we denigrate the perfection of Christ's obedience. As the Heidelberg Catechism, question and answer 61, captures it, we are righteous

16. For this paragraph, see Turretin, *Inst.*, 16.7 (2:669–75); Bavinck, *RD*, 4:209–10; Vos, *Reformed Dogmatics*, 4:152; Hodge, *Systematic Theology*, 3:170–71; Petrus van Mastricht, *Theoretical-Practical Theology*, trans. Todd M. Rester, ed. Joel R. Beeke, 7 vols. (Grand Rapids: Reformation Heritage, 2018–), 2:18–19.

17. The Socinians infamously denied many crucial tenets of orthodox theology, such as the Trinity, the deity of Christ, and eternal life under the old covenant.

18. See, e.g., Racovian Catechism 2.2; 5.8–9; see also Turretin, *Inst.*, 16.7.3 (2:669–70); Mastricht, *Theoretical-Practical Theology*, 2:18, 374.

Instrumental Causation versus Efficient Causation

Faith is the *instrumental* cause, not the *efficient* cause, of justification. The *instrumental cause* is the means by which something occurs. The *efficient cause* refers to the one who acts to bring about the result. God is the efficient cause of justification. Christ's righteousness could also be considered the *meritorious cause* of justification.

—See Turretin, *Inst.*, 16.7.5 (2:670); see also Richard A. Muller, *Dictionary of Latin and Greek Theological Terms: Drawn Principally from Protestant Scholastic Theology*, 2nd ed. (Grand Rapids: Baker Academic, 2017), 56–57, 59

by faith not because of the worthiness of our faith, but because "Only Christ's satisfaction, righteousness, and holiness make me right with God," and this we receive by faith alone.

Justification by faith alone provides great comfort, because we'll never be good enough—no matter how holy we become in practice—to meet the standards of divine justice.[19] Yet we can have confidence that our salvation is secure because its stability rests in the work of God in Christ, not ultimately in ourselves. Assurance of salvation comes not from our ability to believe or behave obediently enough, but primarily by looking to Christ.

If faith is an instrument, can we define it further? The elements of saving faith have been defined different ways, but there is widespread agreement that more than bare knowledge

19. See esp. HC, question and answer 62; Bavinck, *RD*, 4:227–29; Bavinck, *Wonderful Works of God*, 447.

is required. Saving faith must include not only bare knowledge of the gospel message but also belief that it is true ("assent") and a personal persuasion ("trust").[20] Saving faith is primarily receptive and involves both our intellect and will.[21] Scripture is clear that there is a type of faith that is not saving faith. There is a type of faith that knows facts, such as the demons have; this is not saving faith (James 2:14, 19). There is a type of faith that does not persevere (see John 8:31); this also is not saving faith. Throughout the New Testament Abraham provides a paradigm for faith (e.g., Rom. 4:1–12; Gal. 3:7–9). Abraham was counted righteous not because of what he did, but by believing in God's word (Gen. 15:6). Abraham was not justified by his own works, but by faith in God.

Admittedly, James 2:24 does state that Abraham was justified by works and not by faith alone. How can both be true? I'll save that question for the discussion of James 2 in the next chapter.

2. Faith in Christ

Second, since faith is the means of justification, the object of our faith is crucial. The focus of saving faith is Christ. We are not saved by our own faithfulness, but by the work of Christ. This is clear throughout the New Testament, where biblical authors often speak of believing *in* Christ (e.g., John 2:11; 6:29; 9:35–38; 12:44; 17:20; Acts 9:42; 11:17; 16:31; 20:21; 24:24; see also Acts 13:38–39; Gal. 2:16; Eph. 1:15; Col. 1:4; 2:5; Philem. 5; 1 John 3:23).

Put starkly, even Abraham was saved by faith in Christ (see Acts 4:12; 10:43; 15:11), though admittedly much more has been revealed in the New Testament era than was revealed to Abraham in his day.

20. See Turretin, *Inst.*, 15.8–10 (2:560–71); Vos, *Reformed Dogmatics*, 4:72–132.
21. Mastricht, *Theoretical-Practical Theology*, 2:5–15. Mastricht is particularly helpful on this question; his discussion of saving faith (forty pages in English) is thorough and balanced.

3. Faith and Union with Christ

To speak of faith *in Christ* is to speak preeminently of *union with Christ* by faith. The centrality of union with Christ is not contrary to the imputation of Christ's righteousness, but is the context for it. Some object to the imputation of Christ's righteousness for justification because of the way that this seems to portray justification in transactional terms. But that's not how imputation of righteousness is best articulated. Instead, imputation of righteousness finds its context in union with Christ. In justification we benefit not from an abstract principle of righteousness, but from the righteousness of Christ himself.

A survey of Reformed theologians helps us see this point clearly. John Murray highlights the personal contours of union with Christ—the righteousness of Christ for justification cannot be separated from Christ himself: "The righteousness of Christ by which we are justified ([Rom.] 5:17, 18, 19) has its abiding embodiment in Christ; it can never be thought of in abstraction from him as a reservoir of merit stored up."[22] Earlier John Calvin recognized "that as long as Christ remains outside of us, and we are separated from him, all that he has suffered and done for the salvation of the human race remains useless and of no value for us."[23] Likewise Francis Turretin is helpful: "So great is the necessity of faith in the matter of salvation that as Christ alone is the cause of salvation, so faith alone is the means and way to Christ. Hence it is celebrated as the bond of our union with Christ because he dwells in us by faith."[24] Herman Bavinck similarly argues: "The whole person of Christ, in both his active and his passive obedience, is the complete

---

22. John Murray, *The Epistle to the Romans*, 2 vols., NICNT (Grand Rapids: Eerdmans, 1959–65), 1:157; see similarly Ferguson, *Whole Christ*, 48–49.

23. John Calvin, *Institutes of the Christian Religion*, ed. John T. McNeill, trans. Ford Lewis Battles, 2 vols., LCC 20–21 (Philadelphia: Westminster, 1960), 3.1.1 (1:537).

24. Turretin, *Inst.*, 15.7.2 (2:559).

guarantee for the entire redemption that God in his grace grants to individual persons, to humanity, and to the world."[25]

Thus, the best articulations of Christ's imputed righteousness appreciate the dangers and artificiality of abstracting Christ's righteousness from Christ himself. Since salvation centers on union with Christ, there is no need to bifurcate the work of Christ from his person. Union with Christ entails the gift of his perfect righteousness for justification. By faith Christ, by the Holy Spirit, applies his perfect, representative obedience salvifically to all who truly believe.[26] Union with Christ is not coldly transactional, but Spiritual, mystical, and personal.[27] Nor does union with Christ mean that justification is transformative; the foundation of justification is always the perfect obedience of Jesus Christ—an alien righteousness, which does not include the obedience of the believer.

Union with Christ does not render the imputation of Christ's righteousness unnecessary; instead, it ensures that the gift of Christ's righteousness is not severed from the person of Christ.[28]

25. Bavinck, RD, 3:380.
26. See Bavinck, RD, 3:523–24, 568–72; Richard B. Gaffin Jr., "The Work of Christ Applied," in Christian Dogmatics: Reformed Theology for the Church Catholic, ed. Michael Allen and Scott R. Swain (Grand Rapids: Baker Academic, 2016), 268–90 (who notes most of these references to Bavinck).
27. See esp. John Murray, Redemption Accomplished and Applied (Grand Rapids: Eerdmans, 1955), 161–73.
28. See also Turretin, Inst., 15.8.9 (2:563).

9

JESUS'S OBEDIENCE
AND OUR OBEDIENCE

n the previous chapter we considered the role of Christ's
obedience in our justification. It remains to consider the role
of believers' own imperfect obedience in light of the perfect
obedience of Jesus. To what degree is it necessary? Or is it
optional since we are saved by grace? These are complicated
but important questions. In what follows I show how Christian
obedience is necessary, though it never rises to the position of
the ground of our acceptance before God.

Sanctification, Jesus's Obedience, and Our Obedience

Sanctification and Transformation

The application of salvation does not only include justification; it also includes the process of growth in holiness—

sanctification.[1] Distinguishing carefully between justification and sanctification is necessary to preserve the uniqueness of Christ's perfect obedience, but also to emphasize the necessity of believers' good works. This is the point where many studies go astray. Too often sanctification is confused with justification, which makes the works of the believer part of the equation for one's standing before God. But to reiterate a key point of this book, the imperfect obedience of sanctification will not suffice to meet the requirement of perfection—complete sinlessness and complete righteousness—that God requires.

However, this does not mean that good works are optional in the Christian life. Here, too, many studies go astray. For the biblical witness is clear that good works are necessary for salvation.[2] We need to speak carefully and with nuance about sanctification. Sanctification is distinct but inseparable from justification.[3] Whereas justification is not transformative, sanctification is. Transformation is therefore necessary for salvation, but this must not be confused in a way that construes the transformation in the individual to be the ground (or part of the ground) for acceptance before God. Instead, the renovation in the individual that produces good works is a necessary fruit of saving, justifying faith.

To say that good works are necessary for salvation is not to say that they are the foundation of salvation or that by reason of their intrinsic value they merit salvation. It is instead to say that they are "required as the means and way for possessing

---

1. Here I focus on the *progressive* aspect of sanctification, as does Turretin, *Inst.*, 17.1.2 (2:689).

2. Reformed theology has consistently been clear on this point. See, e.g., Turretin, *Inst.*, 17.3 (2:702–5); Bavinck, *RD*, 4:255–56; WCF 13.1; 16.2; see also 11.2; Louis Berkhof, *Systematic Theology*, 4th ed. (Grand Rapids: Eerdmans, 1996), 543. Amandus Polanus von Polansdorf organizes all of Christian theology into two parts: faith and good works; see his *Syntagma Theologiae Christianae* (Hanover: Wechel, 1615), esp. §2.1 (p. 130).

3. See Turretin, *Inst.*, 17.1.1–3 (2:689).

salvation."[4] They are not the *cause* of our new birth, but are its *effects*.[5] Our good works don't earn our salvation, but they are like the wake of a boat that marks our voyage in the Christian life. Understanding the logical distinction between justification and sanctification also helps us understand how someone can be granted eternal life even if they have no apparent opportunity, or very slim opportunity, for good works—such as in the case of a deathbed conversion.[6]

The Reality of Good Works

Sanctification is not optional; it is necessary for salvation. This also means that good works are not figments for Christians; they are actually possible. The life of faith entails "confident dependence" and "obedient submission."[7] Though justification is apart from any work a sinner can do, those who are renewed really can do good works that please God.[8]

It's important to understand what constitutes a good work. Though we can admit that even unbelievers, by God's common grace, can do virtuous deeds,[9] properly speaking four things are necessary for works to be truly good:[10]

4. Turretin, *Inst.*, 17.3.3 (2:702); see also 12.3 (2:184–89); 15.5.21 (2:546); 17.5.13 (2:714).

5. Turretin, *Inst.*, 17.3.15 (2:705).

6. Note the caution of Berkhof, *Systematic Theology*, 543.

7. Petrus van Mastricht, *Theoretical-Practical Theology*, trans. Todd M. Rester, ed. Joel R. Beeke, 7 vols. (Grand Rapids: Reformation Heritage, 2018–), 2:39.

8. See WCF 16.6; Turretin, *Inst.*, 16.8.13 (2:680); 17.4.11 (2:708).

9. See, e.g., Herman Bavinck, *Reformed Ethics: Created, Fallen, and Converted Humanity*, ed. John Bolt, 3 vols. (Grand Rapids: Baker Academic, 2019–), 1:155–61; Bavinck, *RD*, 4:256–57.

10. Following Turretin, *Inst.*, 17.4.5 (2:706); WCF 16; see also HC, question and answer 91; Bavinck, *RD*, 4:256. See also the chart on good works in Zacharias Ursinus, *The Commentary of Dr. Zacharias Ursinus on the Heidelberg Catechism*, trans. G. W. Williard, 2nd ed. (Columbus, OH: Scott & Bascom, 1852), 479. Thanks to Todd Rester for this reference.

1. Truly good works must be done by those who have been justified and renewed in Christ. No work of a sinner is perfectly good, and thus no such work is the basis for acceptance before God. Further, even good works of redeemed sinners are always imperfect. And yet God is pleased to accept the good works of those who are in Christ, who atones for our good works.[11]

2. Good works are only those that are commanded in Scripture. Thus, no person can bind another person's conscience by requiring something not required by Scripture. This is an important point today, for there are many worthwhile causes in the world and many ways to apply Scripture's command to love your neighbor as yourself. It is probably true that, given today's connected world, we are now aware of more worthwhile causes, needs, and injustices to address than previous generations. The command to love our neighbor is non-negotiable. But *how* we love our neighbor—where we invest our time, prayers, resources, and energy—may vary from one person to the next. The church comprises people with a wonderful diversity of gifts and callings, so that what might be a good and proper application of the commands of Scripture for one person might be different for another. No person can require another person to do something or participate in something as *necessary* if that activity is not commanded in Scripture. The moral law of God is actually quite flexible in terms of how it is to be applied.

3. Good works are not merely external deeds, but are done with proper motives. The law of God is spiritual and concerned with the heart and not only external actions. This means, for example, that it is not right to give to

11. See Bavinck, *Reformed Ethics*, 1:154; WCF 16.6.

the work of the Lord while grumbling, for God loves a cheerful giver (2 Cor. 9:7).

4. Good works are done to the glory of God.

Thus, good works of believers are truly good, but they are never inherently good enough to be accepted before the tribunal of God. We can never stand before God on the basis of our own works—even our works of true Christian obedience. Even the most holy in this life realize only the beginnings of the obedience that is truly required.[12] The "evangelical obedience" of believers (that is, "Christian obedience") never suffices for justification. In that sense, our works will always be "filthy rags" (Isa. 64:6 KJV).[13] Even so, "filthy rags" is not the *only* category we need to understand our works. Since the message of salvation includes sanctification along with justification (and thus assumes the reality of our good works), "filthy rags" does not adequately describe the lawful works done by those in Christ with the right motivation and for the proper ends.

In sum, it is a mistake to think that sinful human works can provide an adequate foundation for justification. But it is also a mistake to think that true Christians can never do anything that pleases God. This leads to a lack of motivation in the Christian life and can open the door to antinomianism. Our good works really can be good; they are not merely filthy rags. Good works are not only possible but necessary. This requires further comment.

Necessity of Good Works

By this point it should be clear why good works do not suffice for justification—no sinful work is ever sufficient. This is why the obedience of Christ is indispensable. So when I argue that

---

12. HC, question and answer 114; see also HC, question and answer 62.
13. See Mastricht, *Theoretical-Practical Theology*, 2:401, 416.

good works are necessary for salvation, this does *not* mean that they are the *basis upon* which anyone can be accepted before God. Instead, they are necessary, as we have seen, as the means and way of salvation.

Despite the rigor with which Reformational theology resists the idea that any sinner's works are sufficient to withstand the judgment of God for justification, it would be a colossal misunderstanding to conclude that good works are in any way *optional* or somehow *unimportant*. By no means! Justification and sanctification have to be understood as a package deal; one does not experience one without the other. Turretin states the matter bluntly: "No one is justified by Christ who is not also sanctified and gifted with inherent righteousness."[14] And again, "No one can be glorified in heaven who has not been sanctified on earth by the pursuit of holiness and obedience to the law."[15] Justification and sanctification are both necessary, but they are not to be confused.

Through Christ we are freed from the burden of perfect obedience to the law; yet we are never absolved from our obligation to obey the law. Our obedience remains important and necessary, but only Jesus's obedience withstands the judgment of God. Even if we do all that is required, we will never merit eternal life. We will remain unworthy servants.[16] The life of faith is thus a life of obedience.

Judgment according to Works

Though our works are not the foundation for justification, the Bible does speak about the final judgment in relation to our works. Here, as with so many of the topics in this chapter, we need to be exceptionally careful. Much debate has ensued on the role of our works in the final judgment. It is crucial that we

14. Turretin, *Inst.*, 16.3.10 (2:649).
15. Turretin, *Inst.*, 11.23.6 (2:143).
16. Turretin, *Inst.*, 17.5.20 (2:716); Bavinck, *RD*, 2:570; WCF 16.5.

remember what I have argued thus far: that only Christ's perfect obedience meets the demands for eternal life. The foundation for our standing before God is only the righteousness of Christ.

But if this is the case, then what do we make of all the texts in Scripture that speak about God judging our works?[17] And why does Paul say that it is the *doers* of the law who will be justified (Rom. 2:13)? Such texts can mean neither that our works are the foundation for justification nor that our works are unimportant. Crucially, the Bible speaks not of judgment *based on* (*dia*) our works, but judgment *according to* (*kata*) our works.[18] There is a slight, but significant, distinction between these phrases. Though the foundation of our justification is the perfect obedience of Jesus Christ, God's righteous judgment will be *consistent with* (i.e., "according to") our works. God is even pleased to reward the works of his people. Yet rewards are not due to the inherent value of our works, but to the grace of God. For even our ability to do good works is a gift. When Paul says in Romans 2:13 that the doers of the law will be justified, he has in view either the impossibility of being justified by the law or the reality that those who are justified are sanctified as well. Either way, he does not teach that our works are the foundation for our justification (see 3:20).

New Testament Emphasis on Sanctification

The New Testament often emphasizes the necessity of sanctification. I will discuss briefly four texts: 1 Corinthians 6, Ephesians 2, Philippians 2, and James 2. These texts attest the biblical

---

17. E.g., Acts 17:31; 24:25; Rom. 2:6, 16; 14:9–12; 1 Cor. 3:13–15; 4:5; 2 Cor. 5:10; 2 Tim. 4:1, 8.

18. E.g., Rom. 2:6; 2 Cor. 11:15; 2 Tim. 4:14; Rev. 2:23; 22:12. See further Herman N. Ridderbos, *Paul: An Outline of His Theology*, trans. John Richard De Witt (Grand Rapids: Eerdmans, 1975), 178–81; Richard B. Gaffin Jr., *By Faith, Not by Sight: Paul and the Order of Salvation* (Waynesboro, GA: Paternoster, 2006), 98–99; Turretin, *Inst.*, 17.5.26 (2:719); 20.6.20 (3:603).

dynamic between the *indicative* and the *imperative*.[19] The indicative refers to the saving facts of salvation—the work of Christ that provides the foundation for our justification. The imperative correlates to sanctification and cannot be separated from the indicative. This indicative-imperative dynamic resembles the relationship between justification and sanctification: they are inseparable but cannot be confused. Both are necessary; justification by faith alone does not negate the consistent emphasis in the New Testament on the nonnegotiable nature of practical holiness.

1 Corinthians 6

One text to consider is 1 Corinthians 6:9–11:

> Or do you not know that the unrighteous will not inherit the kingdom of God? Do not be deceived: neither the sexually immoral, nor idolaters, nor adulterers, nor men who practice homosexuality, nor thieves, nor the greedy, nor drunkards, nor revilers, nor swindlers will inherit the kingdom of God. And such were some of you. But you were washed, you were sanctified, you were justified in the name of the Lord Jesus Christ and by the Spirit of our God.

In 6:9a Paul states a principle: the unrighteous (*adikoi*) will not inherit the kingdom of God. Paul soon discusses justification by faith alone (6:11), but the truth of 6:9a must not be dismissed or treated as hypothetical. The Scriptures consistently teach that the unrighteous will not inherit the kingdom of God.[20] In 6:9b–10 Paul illustrates the type of unrighteousness he has in view in 6:9a, before reminding the Corinthians of the effects of the gospel among them in 6:11: "But you were washed, but

---

19. See Ridderbos, *Paul*, 253–58; Gaffin, *By Faith, Not by Sight*, 68–75, 131.
20. E.g., Rom. 1:18–32; Gal. 5:19–21; Eph. 5:3–7; Col. 3:5–8; 1 Thess. 4:3–8; Titus 3:3–7; Rev. 21:8; 22:14–15; see also 1 Tim. 1:8–10; 2 Tim. 3:1–9; 1 Pet. 4:1–5.

you were sanctified, but you were justified [*edikaiōthēte*] in the name of the Lord Jesus Christ and by the Spirit of our God." In 6:11 Paul speaks of the transition of the Corinthians from darkness to light: they were washed from their sins (see Eph. 5:26; Titus 3:5); they were justified and freed from condemnation; they were sanctified and set apart as holy. This sanctification is best taken as a once-for-all sanctification, sometimes called "definitive sanctification." Definitive sanctification refers to the decisive break with the power and realm of sin, a break which comes through union by faith with the crucified and resurrected Christ (see also Rom. 6:2–11).[21] Yet definitive sanctification is the wellspring for good works; it does not negate the need for progressive sanctification—or growth in holiness—as the vice list in 1 Corinthians 6:9–10 warns.

This passage shows in short scope two corresponding realities. On the one hand, by being washed, justified, and (definitively) sanctified, the Corinthian Christians were cleansed from past sins like those listed in 1 Corinthians 6:9b–10. At the same time, if anyone—even among those who profess to be Christians—were to live in accord with the vice list of 6:9b–10, then they would not inherit the kingdom of God (see 2 Pet. 1:5–9). Yet this warning does not undermine the freedom granted in justification, nor does it contradict justification by faith alone apart from works. Neither does it mean that one could be truly justified and then lose that justification. It does mean, however, that those who are justified by faith must manifest the truth and vitality of their faith by walking in a manner pleasing to and submissive to God. One's profession of faith in Christ must be accompanied by growth in holiness. Paul emphasizes both aspects: those who live unrighteously will not inherit the kingdom of God, and God justifies sinners by faith alone apart from any works they could do.

21. See the classic essay by John Murray, "Definitive Sanctification," *CTJ* 2 (1967): 5–21.

Ephesians 2

In Ephesians 2:1–9 Paul extols the mercy and grace of God (2:4–5, 8–9), who made us alive with Christ even when we were spiritually dead in our trespasses and sins (2:1, 5). He saved us even when we were by nature under the wrath of God (2:3). Justification is necessary to be delivered from the wrath of God. Paul provides one of the most striking and succinct statements of justification by faith alone in Ephesians 2:8–9: "For by grace you have been saved through faith. And this is not your own doing; it is the gift of God, not a result of works, so that no one may boast." Paul thus emphasizes the vivifying grace of God in contrast to our deadness and inability, which are due to our own sin. Here the "works" (*erga*) that are unable to save are clearly *any* human works[22]—the debated phrase "works of the law," which some argue pertains to a few, specific works of the law, is not used. Our standing before God is not due in any part to anything we could do. Ephesians 2:1–9 is about justification—being made spiritually alive and delivered from God's wrath. We are justified by grace through faith alone, not by any work done by us.

But we must keep reading. Justification apart from works is closely tied to sanctification. In the next verse (Eph. 2:10) Paul states that although we are not saved *by* good works, we are saved *for* good works (see 1:4). Only after being renewed and saved by grace can we truly embark on a path of good works. Good works are imperative for the Christian (see especially Eph. 4–6), even though sinners are entirely incapable of meriting eternal life on the basis of those good works. They are instead the evidence of true, justifying faith. This manifests the indicative-imperative structure of Paul's theology.

22. See Thomas R. Schreiner, *New Testament Theology: Magnifying God in Christ* (Grand Rapids: Baker Academic, 2008), 527.

Philippians 2

A similar dynamic is evident in Philippians 2:12–13:

> Therefore, my beloved, as you have always obeyed, so now, not only as in my presence but much more in my absence, work out your own salvation with fear and trembling, for it is God who works in you, both to will and to work for his good pleasure.

Paul encourages the Philippians to work out their salvation with fear and trembling. This working out requires effort and living consistently with the truth of the gospel, which follows the pattern of Christ (see Phil. 2:5–11). This is possible because it is God who works in his people. We have seen that in Philippians 3 Paul himself renounces his own righteousness and looks to the righteousness that comes from God by faith (3:9). Paul knows he must press forward to the goal of the resurrection before him (3:13). At the same time, his effort is not antithetical to the divine work of grace in him. Paul strove forward by grace, recognizing that his standing came from God and not from his own works.

James 2

We saw earlier that Abraham was justified by faith, not by works. And yet James 2:24 states: "You see that a person is justified by works and not by faith alone." To understand what this means, we need, first of all, to appreciate the importance of true, saving faith in the Epistle of James and the letter's focus on sanctification rather than on justification. We also need to appreciate that not every usage of the term *justify* means exactly the same thing in the Bible.

Justification by grace through faith is assumed in James (see 1:18, 21), but the emphasis is more on the need for Christian obedience. James 2:24 points out that not all those who claim to have faith truly have saving faith (2:18–20). This underscores what we saw earlier: not all faith is saving faith. In James 2 the difference between saving faith and insufficient faith is particularly in view. James is not out of accord with Paul's teaching in Galatians 2:16—that justification comes by faith apart from works of the law—but James emphasizes that true, saving faith is a faith that works. If someone *claims* to have true faith but that faith produces no good works, it is dead (2:26). True, living faith by definition produces good works. Turretin is characteristically pithy on this topic: "For as faith justifies a person, so works justify faith."[23]

This sampling of texts is illustrative of the New Testament's emphasis on sanctification. Justification apart from our works does not negate the necessity of the believer's good works in sanctification. Salvation requires both.

Living Faithfully in Light of Christ's Faithfulness

The perfect work of Christ, therefore, does not absolve us from the need for practical obedience. Though Jesus's obedience alone is the basis for our justification, ongoing obedience is necessary for those who follow Christ. Justification and sanctification are both necessary for final salvation.

Thankfully, we are not left to guess what is required of us. Paul devotes much space to addressing practical matters. James is almost entirely devoted to practical matters. The New Testament provides ample guidance for how we are to live. The New Testament authors show us how we ought to live in light of the finished work of Christ. But they also do so in light of the law of God from the Old Testament. This means that it's not only in the New Testament where we find direction for

23. Turretin, *Inst.*, 16.8.3 (2:676); see also 16.8.22 (2:682).

how we ought to live; we also look to the law of God in the Old Testament, which continues to be the rule for righteous living in the present age. This requires further comment, which I will provide below.

In what follows we will look first at some necessary context for obedience. Second, we'll look at the law of God. Third, we will relate all these to Christ himself.

Framework for Obedience

It's important that we don't play obedience and faith off against one another. To believe rightly is to obey. This may be part of what Paul means by "the obedience of faith" (*hypakoēn pisteōs*) at the beginning and end of Romans (Rom. 1:5; 16:26). By this Paul may mean the obedience that consists in faith, or perhaps the obedience that flows from faith. Either way, it is not possible to obey apart from faith, nor is it possible to believe apart from obedience. Obedience requires faith, and faith yields obedience. Without faith it is impossible to please God (Heb. 11:6). Our actions matter; we must obey the gospel—the same gospel in which we are to believe (see 1 Cor. 15:1–2; 1 Pet. 4:17).[24] Though our good works do not establish our standing before God, true faith will yield good works.

Any good work must be done to the glory of God (1 Cor. 10:31; see also Col. 3:23). Further, any good work is a work of grace in us. This does not mean it doesn't take effort; sanctification requires intentional, disciplined work (2 Pet. 1:5–9; see also 1 Cor. 15:10; Col. 1:10). We must make every effort to grow in holiness, utilizing the means of grace given to us (e.g., the Word, sacraments, prayer). Even so, we cannot take credit for our good works; all glory goes to God, who works in us by his grace (Phil. 2:12–13).

24. See also Thomas R. Schreiner, *1–2 Peter, Jude*, NAC 37 (Nashville: Broadman & Holman, 2003), 228.

Good works are fruits of the Holy Spirit's work in us. Paul speaks in Galatians 5:22–23 of the fruit of the (Holy) Spirit: "love, joy, peace, patience, kindness, goodness, faithfulness, gentleness and self-control" (NIV 1984). These are indicative of the sorts of actions characterized by those in Christ, who are led by the Spirit. Paul says even more about the life controlled by the Spirit in Romans 8. God's children are led by God's Spirit (Rom. 8:4–17). Romans 8:3–4 is particularly powerful:

> For God has done what the law, weakened by the flesh, could not do. By sending his own Son in the likeness of sinful flesh and for sin, he condemned sin in the flesh, in order that the righteous requirement of the law might be fulfilled in us, who walk not according to the flesh but according to the Spirit.

Though on the one hand, no sinner can fulfill the law for justification, on the other hand, those who are renewed and in Christ fulfill the righteous requirement of the law by walking according to the Spirit. Noting the apparent incongruity between the law's impotence to save in texts like Romans 6:14; 8:3, along with Paul's positive view of the law in 8:4, John Murray concludes that for Paul "the law of God has the fullest normative relevance in that state which is the product of grace."[25] In other words, Paul speaks here of the transformed life that obeys God's law;[26] the law continues to be a guide for righteous living for the redeemed, and those who are led by the Spirit are enabled to fulfill the law's requirement.

Law of God

To say that the law of God continues to be the guide for righteous living requires further comment. For surely the re-

25. John Murray, *The Epistle to the Romans*, 2 vols., NICNT (Grand Rapids: Eerdmans, 1959–65), 1:283.
26. See also Thomas R. Schreiner, *Romans*, 2nd ed., BECNT (Grand Rapids: Baker Academic, 2018), 401.

lationship of believers to the law in the new covenant era is not exactly the same as the relationship of believers in the old covenant era. This is why it is necessary to distinguish between moral, ceremonial, and civil aspects of God's law. Though this construal has often been critiqued, and there is a real danger of making artificial distinctions, it remains the best way to understand how God's law does and does not apply to Christians today.

In short, the moral aspects of God's law remain binding, whereas civil and ceremonial aspects of God's law were given for a temporary purpose and are no longer in effect. This means, for example, it would be wrong to offer perpetual sacrifices for sin, now that Christ has come and offered the final, definitive sacrifice (see Heb. 9:26; 10:11–12). Similarly, civil laws were given to guide Israel as a theocratic nation, but those laws ceased to be in effect for the scattered Jewish people in the New Testament era who lived under foreign rule. The moral aspects of the law, on the other hand, continue to guide and bind us in the new covenant era.

Where do we find the moral law? As I argued earlier, the most concise answer is in the Ten Commandments, which are a summary of the moral law of God. We saw in Hebrews 10 that often the problem was not that God's people didn't keep the ceremonial law, but that they did not offer true obedience from the heart. Recall that one mark of a truly good work is that it proceeds from the proper motives. The Ten Commandments are spiritual and require a deeper application than only a surface-level reading. When Hebrews speaks of the law being written on our hearts in the new covenant, it must refer to the moral aspects of the law (i.e., the Ten Commandments), since the final sacrifice has come and we do not live in a theocracy.[27] Even so,

27. See Sinclair B. Ferguson, *The Whole Christ: Legalism, Antinomianism, and Gospel Assurance—Why the Marrow Controversy Still Matters* (Wheaton: Crossway, 2016), 145.

the *entire* law of God (including ceremonial and civil dimensions) continues to instruct us in what God requires, even if we no longer live under it as a governing covenant administration.

In sum, if we want to grow in holiness and good works, we must seek to obey the Ten Commandments by the power of God's Spirit. The Ten Commandments are not simply prohibitive, but entail positive requirements of what we are obligated to do. The New Testament writers do not so much provide entirely new commandments as they build on and clarify God's law in light of the coming of Christ. In this regard, they often build on the Ten Commandments to show what is positively required.

For example, keeping the Sabbath means not only avoiding certain things, but doing good (Matt. 12:12; Mark 3:4; Luke 6:9). In the Sermon on the Mount Jesus shows how we must not simply avoid murder, but must seek to live at peace (Matt. 5:21–26). Paul shows a similar approach: not only must we *not* steal; we must positively work to provide for those in need (Eph. 4:28). I observed earlier that Paul even quotes the fifth commandment ("Honor your father and your mother") as a command that is still in effect, along with a reward for obedience (6:2–3). In Jesus's six antitheses in the Sermon on the Mount (Matt. 5:21–48), perhaps four of them expound the Ten Commandments.[28] Two of these antitheses focus on the prohibition against adultery (5:27–32), which reflects the particular attention given to sexual sin in the New Testament (e.g., Acts 15:20; Rom. 1:24–27; 1 Cor. 6:9–11; Eph. 4:19–20; 5:3–6; Col. 3:5–6; 1 Thess. 4:3–8; 1 Pet. 4:3; 2 Pet. 2:1–22; Jude 4, 7–8). The Ten Commandments and the Sermon on the Mount show us how far we fall short of God's standards of holiness. But they do more than that; they also provide practical guidance for how God's renewed people are to live in this age—as holy people

28. These echo the prohibitions against murder (Matt. 5:21–26), adultery (5:27–32), and taking God's name in vain (5:33–37).

set apart to the Lord. In sum, we are to be holy, for God is holy (1 Pet. 1:15–16; 2:9–10).

The moral law can also be summarized in the twofold love command: love for God and love for neighbor (Matt. 22:37–40; Mark 12:29–31; Luke 10:27; Rom. 13:8–10; Gal. 5:14; see also Matt. 7:12; James 2:8; possibly Rom. 8:4). To focus on love is not different than focusing on the Ten Commandments, for the call to love is inherent to the Ten Commandments. To believe is to obey, and to obey is to love.

Christ-Focused

Those who are in Christ are therefore freed from the condemnation of the law, but not from the moral constraints of the law. Paul speaks of those who are in Christ as under the law of Christ (1 Cor. 9:21). The "law of Christ" likely points to the summary of the law that Christ gave us (love for God and neighbor) and that Christ himself shows us in practice. Christ's work on earth was one of entire, perfect obedience. He perfectly loved God and perfectly obeyed. He is the blessed man who delighted fully in the law of God (Ps. 1).

To understand what it means to love God and neighbor, we should look to Christ. He brings a new command—that we love one another (John 13:34; see also 1 John 2:7–8). Yet this new command is old, coming from the Old Testament itself (Lev. 19:18). In what sense is it new? It is new in the way that Christ has shown us what it means to love and fulfilled it by laying down his life that his people might live. We obey the law in light of the work of Christ, following in his steps as the one who saves us from the curse of the law and frees us to obey the law (see Gal. 5:1). And if we are in Christ, then the entire context for our obedience is union with Christ. There is no abstraction from Christ himself in our call to obedience; we live with respect to Christ (2:20). Jesus Christ himself shows us how to avoid hypocrisy, loving God fully from the heart and loving our neighbors as ourselves. To delight in Christ is to delight in the law of God; for Christ himself delighted in the law of God. His obedience saves us from our sins and provides a pattern for holiness and obedience to show us what it means to live faithfully in this world. We must follow him each day.

Practically, this means in our efforts toward greater holiness we should look to Christ himself. He is not only our Savior but our model—the truly obedient human being. Consider the way he lived a holy life in the midst of a sinful world. Read the Old Testament law (and the Psalms) with reference to the person and work of Christ. Ask Christ himself to strengthen you by his Spirit. Pray the Lord's Prayer, asking to be spared temptation as you take your stand in Christ himself, who withstood temptation on our account. He has obeyed perfectly so that we are freed to obey—even if imperfectly.

A Call to Persevere

The good news of the free grace of the gospel of Jesus Christ includes the good news that salvation is secure for all those who are in Christ. True believers will never fall away, for their salvation is secure in Christ, by the will of God, for the seed of the Holy Spirit abides in them.[29] Bavinck argues, "It is not just a handful of texts that teach the perseverance of the saints: the entire gospel sustains and confirms it. The Father has chosen them before the foundation of the world (Eph. 1:4), ordained them to eternal life (Acts 13:48), to be conformed to the image of his Son (Rom. 8:29)."[30]

Yet true faith is also persevering faith, as Scripture makes clear. Continued obedience is the means of perseverance.[31] God's control over salvation does not render human obedience negligible. This is one way we see the mysterious interplay

29. See WCF 17.1–2.
30. Bavinck, *RD*, 4:269.
31. Compare Turretin, *Inst.*, 15.16.35 (2:611–12); Bavinck, *RD*, 4:266–70.

between God's sovereignty and human responsibility: God is in control of salvation, but we must continue to believe. This means we must continue to obey. Even so, our hope for the future rests not on ourselves, but on God's promises and the faithfulness of our Savior.

Hebrews addresses this issue at length. The nature of saving faith is by definition *persevering* faith (see Heb. 3:6, 14).[32] Saving faith is persevering faith, and persevering faith is obedient faith. The warnings in Hebrews are particularly poignant in the way they warn those in God's new covenant community against turning back from following Christ (see 2:1–3). The new covenant has truly come, but as it was in the old covenant, so it is in the new: many of those who participate in the covenant community lack true, saving faith (see 3:7–4:13; 6:4–6; 10:26–31). We must not turn back from following Christ. To do so is to shipwreck the faith (see 1 Tim. 1:19). The danger is to turn back when obeying becomes too costly (see 1 Cor. 10:1–13; Heb. 10:32–39; 1 Pet. 4:7–19). To be clear, the New Testament does not teach that true believers can lose their salvation, but it may look that way from a human point of view. The wilderness generation's wayward example in Hebrews is a warning for us, for the gospel was preached to them just as it is to us today (Heb. 4:2). Perseverance in faith is key, even when we face opposition (see Matt. 10:24–25; Acts 14:22; 2 Tim. 3:12; Rev. 1:9). Difficulties should not surprise us; the call is to persevere and follow Christ even when it is difficult (Rev. 13:10; 14:12).

We must therefore press on in holiness toward the future, keeping the final goal in front of us as we follow Christ. In fact, the goal is Christ himself—that we may share in both his suffering and his resurrection (Phil. 3:7–16). Let us follow Paul's example, treating life like a race with a goal in view (Acts 20:24; 1 Cor. 9:24–27; Phil 3:14; see also 2 Tim. 2:5; Heb. 12:1–2).

---

32. I owe this point to D. A. Carson.

Though Christ saves us from the curse of sin, sin continues to be dangerous. No sin is small; every sin would lead us one step further down the path toward apostasy. Obedience is not an abstract idea, but involves decisions we must make each day to follow Christ, even when it is tough in the midst of an ungodly world. Sin is often easier, but it does not lead to blessing. Sin leads to cursing and death; obedience leads to life (James 1:12–15).

Perseverance may sound abstract, but it is a matter for us to consider each day. What will we do *today*? Today let us continue to believe and obey. We're not sure what the future will be, but whatever the future brings, may we be found following Christ: "Here is a call for the endurance of the saints, those who keep the commandments of God and their faith in Jesus" (Rev. 14:12).

10

WHAT IS REQUIRED IS FINISHED

Eternal life requires perfect obedience, and this has been realized by Jesus Christ. So great is his love that the eternal Son of God became incarnate and suffered, obeying the law of God perfectly as a fully human representative. And this he did not for his own sake, but for ours. Jesus's perfect obedience is the foundation for our standing before God. He did what we could never do. He grants what we could never earn.

It has not been my intention to state anything substantially new in this book. Rather my aim has been to show the logic and coherence of the biblical teaching that Jesus's perfect obedience is necessary for salvation. The Reformed tradition from which I write appreciates the goodness of the law of God, the reality of sin, the importance of a Mediator who is fully God and fully man, the forensic reality of justification by faith alone, the necessity of sanctification, and the real call to persevere.

We must not bifurcate between the life and death of Christ; his obedience is an integrated whole. Justification is not impersonal and transactional, but finds its context in union with Christ—the fully obedient one. To be accepted before God requires our sins to be forgiven and for us to be viewed positively as righteous. These requirements have been met on our behalf by Jesus Christ. Though Christian obedience is a real requirement, no sinner's obedience ever suffices—even partly—for justification. Only on the basis of Christ's righteousness can we stand justified before God.

This interpretation of Scripture has a long history. The comforting synthesis of the Heidelberg Catechism (1563) on the matter of justification remains biblically faithful, as it highlights the perfection of Christ's work on our behalf:

Q. How are you right with God?

A. Only by true faith in Jesus Christ. Even though my conscience accuses me of having grievously sinned against all God's commandments and of never having kept any of them, and even though I am still inclined toward all evil, nevertheless, without my deserving it all, out of sheer grace, God grants and credits to me the perfect satisfaction, righteousness, and holiness of Christ, as if I had never sinned nor been a sinner, as if I had been as perfectly obedient as Christ was obedient for me. All I need to do is to accept this gift of God with a believing heart.

The basis (or foundation) of our acceptance before God is the obedience of Christ; faith is the means by which we benefit from his work. Only Christ's obedience is sufficient to meet the strict demands of perfect holiness required by the law of God.

But we don't simply need something *from* Christ; we need Christ himself. The benefits he has acquired are never separated from his person. Herman Bavinck channels the Heidelberg Catechism in his own words:

> The righteousness which justifies us, therefore, is not to be separated from the person of Christ. . . . There is no possibility of sharing in the benefits of Christ without being in fellowship with the person of Christ. . . . In order to stand before the judgment of God, to be acquitted of all guilt and punishment, and to share in the glory of God and eternal life, we must have Christ, not something of Him, but Christ Himself. . . . The crucified and glorified Christ is the righteousness which God grants us through grace in the [*sic*] justification. . . . And then we can stand before His presence as though we had never had sin, or done sin, indeed, as though we had ourselves achieved the obedience which Christ has achieved for us.[1]

The obedience of Christ is not to be separated from Christ himself; for Christ himself is our hope of eternal life.

There is much more that can be said; I have only provided a sketch. But sometimes a sketch can be helpful for getting a sense of the whole.

I conclude with a few observations.

1. To answer the question of whether eternal life requires perfect obedience, we must start at the beginning. This is a question about Adam—about the historical Adam—and not simply a question about Israel. If we don't start at the beginning, our conclusions will be skewed.

2. We must have an appropriately nuanced understanding of the law of God. In the New Testament *law* (*nomos*) often refers to the Mosaic law, but this is not always the case. The law can be viewed from different angles, and New Testament

---

1. Herman Bavinck, *The Wonderful Works of God: Instruction in the Christian Religion according to the Reformed Confession*, trans. Henry Zylstra (repr., Philadelphia: Westminster Seminary Press, 2019), 436; see also Bavinck, *RD*, 4:263.

writers emphasize the law in various ways, depending on the point they wish to make. The law is good and is a guide for righteous living. Perfect obedience is not necessary for covenant members to live faithfully after the fall. But the law also attests the abiding principle that eternal life requires perfect obedience; what is good can become a snare to those who seek to live by works instead of by faith.

3. Central to justification is the perfect, representative obedience of Christ. The faith of the believer is in no way the basis of justification, nor is faith properly a work. Instead, faith is the instrument by which we benefit from Christ's perfect obedience, and his obedience alone is the basis for our justification. By faith we are united to Christ himself. We are not justified in any way based on what we can or will do, but only on the basis of Christ's perfect obedience.

4. Justification apart from works does not free believers from the need for true obedience. Sanctification, while distinct from justification, is necessary and inseparable from justification. Although imperfect works do not suffice for justification, they are accepted in Christ and necessary for final salvation.

5. A satisfactory theology of Jesus's obedience does not come from only one biblical text or one author, but from the canon as a whole. To articulate the importance of Jesus's obedience requires us to take the full range of biblical evidence into consideration, and we must relate these texts with nuance, thoroughness, and logical coherence. In other words, to answer the questions in this volume requires synthesis and organization. That means it is prudent to use the tools and insights of systematic theology to help us make sense of a diverse array of biblical texts, to speak clearly with respect to a diversity of voices. We need precise, technical language to communicate the precious truths of the good news of Jesus Christ. We also need to value the collective wisdom of those who have wrestled with these important questions before us.

In the end, our hope is not in ourselves, but in Christ and what he has done for us. Not only does Jesus provide the quintessential model for obedience in a fallen world, but more than that, his obedience actually saves. We must therefore look outside ourselves to Jesus—the founder and perfecter of our faith who has gone before us and defeated sin and death. Our life is found in him. For by one man's obedience we have been freed from the burden of perfect obedience and the curse that comes to all who fail to meet that standard. By one man's obedience we have been redeemed by grace through faith. Though death comes by disobedience, we are freely granted eternal life that has been secured by one man's obedience.

BIBLIOGRAPHY

Bates, Matthew W. *Salvation by Allegiance Alone: Rethinking Faith, Works, and the Gospel of Jesus the King*. Grand Rapids: Baker Academic, 2017.

Bavinck, Herman. *Reformed Dogmatics*. Edited by John Bolt. Translated by John Vriend. 4 vols. Grand Rapids: Baker Academic, 2003–8.

———. *Reformed Ethics: Created, Fallen, and Converted Humanity*. Edited by John Bolt. 3 vols. Grand Rapids: Baker Academic, 2019–.

———. *The Wonderful Works of God: Instruction in the Christian Religion according to the Reformed Confession*. Translated by Henry Zylstra. Repr., Philadelphia: Westminster Seminary Press, 2019.

Beale, G. K. *A New Testament Biblical Theology: The Unfolding of the Old Testament in the New*. Grand Rapids: Baker Academic, 2011.

Beale, G. K., and Benjamin L. Gladd. *The Story Retold: A Biblical Theological Introduction to the New Testament*. Downers Grove, IL: IVP Academic, 2020.

Berkhof, Louis. *Systematic Theology*. 4th ed. Grand Rapids: Eerdmans, 1996.

Best, Ernest. *The Temptation and the Passion: The Markan Soteriology*. 2nd ed. SNTSMS 2. Cambridge: Cambridge University Press, 1990.

Bock, Darrell L. *Luke*. 2 vols. BECNT. Grand Rapids: Baker, 1994–96.

Bruce, F. F. *The Epistle to the Hebrews*. NICNT. Grand Rapids: Eerdmans, 1964.

Calvin, John. *Commentaries on the Epistle of Paul the Apostle to the Romans*. Translated by John Owen. Repr., Grand Rapids: Baker, 2003.

———. *Commentaries on the Epistles of Paul to the Galatians and Ephesians*. Translated by William Pringle. Repr., Grand Rapids: Baker, 2003.

———. *Institutes of the Christian Religion*. Edited by John T. McNeill. Translated by Ford Lewis Battles. 2 vols. LCC 20–21. Philadelphia: Westminster, 1960.

Carson, D. A. "Matthew." In *Matthew, Mark, Luke*, vol. 8 of *The Expositor's Bible Commentary*, edited by Frank L. Gaebelein, 1–599. Grand Rapids: Zondervan, 1984.

Crowe, Brandon D. "'By Grace You Have Been Saved through Faith': Justification in the Pauline Epistles." In *The Doctrine on Which the Church Stands or Falls: Justification in Biblical, Theological, Historical, and Pastoral Perspective*, edited by Matthew Barrett, 235–67. Wheaton: Crossway, 2019.

———. "The Chiastic Structure of Seven Signs in the Gospel of John: Revisiting a Neglected Proposal." *BBR* 28 (2018): 65–81.

———. "Fulfillment in Matthew as Eschatological Reversal." *WTJ* 75 (2013): 111–27.

———. *The Hope of Israel: The Resurrection of Christ in the Acts of the Apostles*. Grand Rapids: Baker Academic, 2020.

———. "Jesus, Our Great High Priest." *Credo Magazine* 6, no. 2 (2016): 16–21.

———. *The Last Adam: A Theology of the Obedient Life of Jesus in the Gospels*. Grand Rapids: Baker Academic, 2017.

———. "Oh Sweet Exchange! The Soteriological Significance of the Incarnation in the *Epistle to Diognetus*." *ZNW* 102 (2011): 96–109.

———. "The Passive and Active Obedience of Christ: Recovering a Biblical Distinction." In *The Doctrine on Which the Church Stands or Falls: Justification in Biblical, Theological, Historical, and Pastoral Perspective*, edited by Matthew Barrett, 437–64. Wheaton: Crossway, 2019.

———. *The Path of Faith: A Biblical Theology of Covenant and Law*. ESBT. Downers Grove, IL: IVP Academic, 2021.

———. "Reading Psalm 40 Messianically." *Reformed Faith and Practice* 2, no. 3 (December 2017): 31–44.

———. "Reading the Lord's Prayer Christologically." In *Redeeming the Life of the Mind: Essays in Honor of Vern Sheridan Poythress*, edited by John Frame, Wayne Grudem, and John J. Hughes, 79–96. Wheaton: Crossway, 2017.

Danker, Frederick W., Walter Bauer, William F. Arndt, and F. Wilbur Gingrich. *Greek-English Lexicon of the New Testament and Other Early Christian Literature*. 3rd ed. Chicago: University of Chicago Press, 2000.

De Chirico, Leonardo. "Not by Faith Alone? An Analysis of the Roman Catholic Doctrine of Justification from Trent to the *Joint Declaration*." In *The Doctrine on Which the Church Stands or Falls: Justification in Biblical, Theological, Historical, and Pastoral Perspective*, edited by Matthew Barrett, 739–67. Wheaton: Crossway, 2019.

Dennison, James T., Jr., ed. *Reformed Confessions of the Sixteenth and Seventeenth Centuries in English Translation, 1523–1693*. 4 vols. Grand Rapids: Reformation Heritage, 2008–14.

deSilva, David A. *Perseverance in Gratitude: A Socio-Rhetorical Commentary on the Epistle "to the Hebrews."* Grand Rapids: Eerdmans, 2000.

Ellingworth, Paul. *The Epistle to the Hebrews: A Commentary on the Greek Text*. NIGTC. Grand Rapids: Eerdmans, 1993.

Ferguson, Everett. *The Rule of Faith: A Guide*. Cascade Companions. Eugene, OR: Cascade Books, 2015.

Ferguson, Sinclair B. *The Holy Spirit*. CCT. Downers Grove, IL: InterVarsity, 1996.

———. *The Whole Christ: Legalism, Antinomianism, and Gospel Assurance—Why the Marrow Controversy Still Matters*. Wheaton: Crossway, 2016.

Fitzmyer, Joseph A. *Romans: A New Translation with Introduction and Commentary*. AB 33. New Haven: Yale University Press, 1993.

Gaffin, Richard B., Jr. *By Faith, Not by Sight: Paul and the Order of Salvation*. Waynesboro, GA: Paternoster, 2006.

———. *The Centrality of the Resurrection: A Study in Paul's Soteriology*. Baker Biblical Monographs. Grand Rapids: Baker, 1978.

————. *No Adam, No Gospel: Adam and the History of Redemption.* Phillipsburg, NJ: P&R, 2015.

————. "The Priesthood of Christ: A Servant in the Sanctuary." In *The Perfect Saviour: Key Themes in Hebrews*, edited by Jonathan Griffiths, 49–68. Nottingham: Inter-Varsity, 2012.

————. "The Work of Christ Applied." In *Christian Dogmatics: Reformed Theology for the Church Catholic*, edited by Michael Allen and Scott R. Swain, 268–90. Grand Rapids: Baker Academic, 2016.

Garner, David B. *Sons in the Son: The Riches and Reach of Adoption in Christ.* Phillipsburg, NJ: P&R, 2016.

Geldenhuys, Norval. *Commentary on the Gospel of Luke.* NICNT. Grand Rapids: Eerdmans, 1951.

Gentry, Peter J., and Stephen G. Wellum. *Kingdom through Covenant: A Biblical-Theological Understanding of the Covenants.* 2nd ed. Wheaton: Crossway, 2018.

Girard, Marc. "La composition structurelle des sept 'signes' dans le quatrième évangile." *Studies in Religion/Sciences Religieuses* 9 (1980): 315–24.

Hodge, Charles. *Systematic Theology.* 3 vols. Repr., Peabody, MA: Hendrickson, 2008.

Holmes, Michael W. *The Apostolic Fathers: Greek Texts and English Translations.* 3rd ed. Grand Rapids: Baker Academic, 2007.

Irenaeus. *On the Apostolic Preaching.* Translated by John Behr. PPS. Crestwood, NY: St. Vladimir's Seminary Press, 1997.

Keener, Craig S. *Galatians: A Commentary.* Grand Rapids: Baker Academic, 2019.

Koester, Craig R. *Hebrews: A New Translation with Introduction and Commentary.* AB 36. New York: Doubleday, 2001.

Köstenberger, Andreas J. "Translator's Preface." In *The History of the Christ: The Foundation for New Testament Theology*, by Adolf Schlatter, translated by Andreas J. Köstenberger, 14. Grand Rapids: Baker, 1997.

Lane, William L. *Hebrews 1–8.* WBC 47A. Nashville: Nelson, 1991.

————. *Hebrews 9–13.* WBC 47B. Nashville: Nelson, 2000.

Letham, Robert. *The Work of Christ.* CCT. Downers Grove, IL: Inter-Varsity, 1993.

Longenecker, Richard N. "The Obedience of Christ in the Theology of the Early Church." In *Reconciliation and Hope: New Testament Essays on Atonement and Eschatology Presented to L. L. Morris on His 60th Birthday*, edited by Robert Banks, 142–52. Grand Rapids: Eerdmans, 1974.

Luther, Martin. *Luther's Works*. Edited by Jaroslav Pelikan, Helmut T. Lehmann, and Christopher Brown. American ed. 82 vols. (projected). Philadelphia: Fortress; Saint Louis: Concordia, 1955–.

Macaskill, Grant. *Union with Christ in the New Testament*. Oxford: Oxford University Press, 2014.

Macleod, Donald. *Christ Crucified: Understanding the Atonement*. Downers Grove, IL: InterVarsity, 2014.

Mastricht, Petrus van. *Theoretical-Practical Theology*. Translated by Todd M. Rester. Edited by Joel R. Beeke. 7 vols. Grand Rapids: Reformation Heritage, 2018–.

Moffitt, David M. *Atonement and the Logic of Resurrection in the Epistle to the Hebrews*. NovTSup 141. Leiden: Brill, 2011.

Moo, Douglas J. *Galatians*. BECNT. Grand Rapids: Baker Academic, 2013.

Muller, Richard A. *Dictionary of Latin and Greek Theological Terms: Drawn Principally from Protestant Scholastic Theology*. 2nd ed. Grand Rapids: Baker Academic, 2017.

Murray, John. "Definitive Sanctification." *CTJ* 2 (1967): 5–21.

———. *The Epistle to the Romans*. 2 vols. NICNT. Grand Rapids: Eerdmans, 1959–65.

———. *The Imputation of Adam's Sin*. Grand Rapids: Eerdmans, 1959.

———. *Redemption Accomplished and Applied*. Grand Rapids: Eerdmans, 1955.

Owen, John. *ΧΡΙΣΤΟΛΟΓΙΑ: Or, A Declaration of the Glorious Mystery of the Person of Christ*. In *The Glory of Christ*, vol. 1 of *The Works of John Owen*, edited by William H. Goold, 1–272. Edinburgh: Banner of Truth, 1965.

Polanus von Polansdorf, Amandus. *Syntagma Theologiae Christianae*. Hanover: Wechel, 1615.

Rees, Thomas, ed. *The Racovian Catechism, with Notes and Illustrations, Translated from the Latin: To Which Is Prefixed a Sketch of the History of Unitarianism in Poland and the Adjacent Countries.* London: Longman, Hurst, Reese, Orme, and Brown, 1818.

Ribbens, Benjamin J. "The Sacrifice God Desired: Psalm 40:6–8 in Hebrews 10." *NTS* 67 (2021): 284–304.

Ridderbos, Herman N. *Paul: An Outline of His Theology.* Translated by John Richard De Witt. Grand Rapids: Eerdmans, 1975.

Schreiner, Thomas R. *1–2 Peter, Jude.* NAC 37. Nashville: Broadman & Holman, 2003.

———. *Galatians.* ZECNT. Grand Rapids: Zondervan, 2010.

———. *New Testament Theology: Magnifying God in Christ.* Grand Rapids: Baker Academic, 2008.

———. *Romans.* 2nd ed. BECNT. Grand Rapids: Baker Academic, 2018.

Shively, Elizabeth E. *Apocalyptic Imagination in the Gospel of Mark: The Literary and Theological Role of Mark 3:22–30.* BZNW 189. Berlin: de Gruyter, 2012.

Silva, Moisés. "Abraham, Faith, and Works: Paul's Use of Scripture in Galatians 3:6–14." *WTJ* 63 (2001): 251–67.

———. "Faith versus Works of the Law in Galatians." In *The Paradoxes of Paul*, vol. 2 of *Justification and Variegated Nomism*, edited by D. A. Carson, Peter T. O'Brien, and Mark A. Seifrid, 217–48. WUNT 2/181. Repr., Grand Rapids: Baker Academic, 2004.

———. *Interpreting Galatians: Explorations in Exegetical Method.* 2nd ed. Grand Rapids: Baker Academic, 2001.

———. "Perfection and Eschatology in Hebrews." *WTJ* 39 (1976): 60–71.

Snodgrass, Klyne R. *Stories with Intent: A Comprehensive Guide to the Parables of Jesus.* Grand Rapids: Eerdmans, 2008.

Tanner, Norman P., ed. *Decrees of the Ecumenical Councils.* 2 vols. Washington, DC: Georgetown University Press, 1990.

Tipton, Lane G. "Christology in Colossians 1:15–20 and Hebrews 1:1–4: An Exercise in Biblico-Systematic Theology." In *Resurrection and Eschatology: Theology in Service of the Church; Essays in Honor of Richard B. Gaffin Jr.*, edited by Lane G. Tipton and Jeffrey C. Waddington, 177–202. Phillipsburg, NJ: P&R, 2008.

Turretin, Francis. *Institutes of Elenctic Theology.* Edited by James T. Dennison Jr. Translated by George Musgrave Giger. 3 vols. Phillipsburg, NJ: P&R, 1992–97.

Ursinus, Zacharias. *The Commentary of Dr. Zacharias Ursinus on the Heidelberg Catechism*. Translated by G. W. Williard. 2nd ed. Columbus, OH: Scott & Bascom, 1852.

Vos, Geerhardus. *Biblical Theology: Old and New Testaments*. 1948. Repr., Edinburgh: Banner of Truth, 1975.

———. *The Pauline Eschatology*. Grand Rapids: Eerdmans, 1961.

———. *Reformed Dogmatics*. 5 vols. Edited and translated by Richard B. Gaffin Jr. Bellingham, WA: Lexham, 2012–16.

Wright, N. T. *The Climax of the Covenant: Christ and the Law in Pauline Theology*. Minneapolis: Fortress, 1992.

———. *Paul and the Faithfulness of God*. COQG 4. Minneapolis: Fortress, 2013.

———. *Paul: In Fresh Perspective*. Minneapolis: Fortress, 2005.

PERMISSIONS

I would like to thank several publishers in particular for their permissions to reappropriate some previously published material.

Crossway has granted permission to reuse portions of three essays. Given the frequency and diversity in ways in which I engage these essays, I summarize their usage here in lieu of multiple footnotes throughout the book:

"The Passive and Active Obedience of Christ: Recovering a Biblical Distinction," in *The Doctrine on Which the Church Stands or Falls: Justification in Biblical, Theological, Historical, and Pastoral Perspective*, ed. Matthew Barrett (Wheaton: Crossway, 2019), 437–64. I include significant portions from this essay in chapters 2–3, along with chapters 5, 7.

"'By Grace You Have Been Saved through Faith': Justification in the Pauline Epistles," in *The Doctrine on Which the Church Stands or Falls: Justification in Biblical, Theological, Historical, and Pastoral Perspective*, ed. Matthew Barrett (Wheaton: Crossway, 2019), 235–67. I include portions from this essay in chapters 4, 7–9.

"Reading the Lord's Prayer Christologically," in *Redeeming the Life of the Mind: Essays in Honor of Vern Sheridan*

Poythress, ed. John Frame, Wayne Grudem, and John J. Hughes (Wheaton: Crossway, 2017), 79–96. I build on this essay in my discussion of the Lord's Prayer in chapter 5.

Material on the structure of John in chapter 5 is taken from Brandon D. Crowe, "The Chiastic Structure of Seven Signs in the Gospel of John: Revisiting a Neglected Proposal," *BBR* 28 (2018): 65–81, copyright © 2018 by the Pennsylvania State University Press. This article is used by permission of the Pennsylvania State University Press.

Quotations from the Heidelberg Catechism (1563) are taken from the translation adopted by the Christian Reformed Church in 1975 and approved in 1988, available online: https://www .crcna.org/sites/default/files/Heidelberg%20Catechism_old .pdf. Quotations from the Westminster Shorter Catechism, the Westminster Confession of Faith, and the Westminster Larger Catechism, are taken from James T. Dennison Jr., ed., *Reformed Confessions of the Sixteenth and Seventeenth Centuries in English Translation, 1523–1693*, 4 vols. (Grand Rapids: Reformation Heritage, 2008–14).

SCRIPTURE INDEX

SUBJECT INDEX

"Many Christians today understand that Christ had to suffer on our behalf and bear the penalty for our sin, but they have no idea why Jesus also had to live a perfect life. Yet without the active obedience of Christ, how can we be justified before God? With profound biblical and theological insight, Crowe teaches us that we not only need our sins forgiven but also need the spotless righteousness of our Savior. Apart from the imputation of Christ's righteousness, our salvation is incomplete! Here is a book that is not only accessible but timely: in a day when imputation is often rejected, Crowe reveals just how critical Christ's entire life is to our union with Christ. There is no hope without it."

—**Matthew Barrett**, Midwestern Baptist Theological Seminary; host of the *Credo Podcast*

"Some think the imputation of Christ's righteousness is abstract and separated from our everyday lives. Crowe shows that the doctrine is woven into the warp and woof of biblical teaching, and that knowing and cherishing this truth is vital for spiritual life. There is a beautiful simplicity and clarity in this book, which makes it an ideal resource both for young believers and for those who have known the good news for years. We also find here an example of theological interpretation of Scripture that includes the great confessions of the Reformation. The best theological interpretation doesn't restrict itself to the early church but also mines the insights of the Reformation. I hope and pray for a wide reading of this profound book."

—**Thomas R. Schreiner**, Southern Baptist Theological Seminary

"Christians confess that Jesus Christ is an obedient Savior. But why was Jesus's obedience necessary for our salvation? In an accessible survey of biblical passages that reflects careful and insightful handling of Scripture and that converses with some of the best theological minds of the church, Crowe helps us to see that the obedience of Christ is truly good news for sinners. *Why Did Jesus Live a Perfect Life?* will benefit both nonspecialists and scholars as it brings to light an often-neglected but vital line of the New Testament's testimony to Christ."

—**Guy Prentiss Waters**, Reformed Theological Seminary